S0-EAQ-138

SKILLS
FOR
LEADERS

by
John W. Gray
and
Angela Laird Pfeiffer

NATIONAL ASSOCIATION OF SECONDARY SCHOOL PRINCIPALS
RESTON, VIRGINIA

ABOUT THE AUTHORS

John W. Gray and Angela Laird Pfeiffer are both on the faculty of the University of Arkansas at Little Rock. Gray has been on the staff of the National Leadership Training Conferences and is a consultant with NASSP and NASC. Pfeiffer teaches classes in leadership and has conducted seminars for student leadership groups at the high school and college levels.

NASSP Executive Director: Scott D. Thomson
Director, Student Activities: Dale D. Hawley
Director, Publications
   and Editorial Services: Thomas F. Koerner
Editor: Jackie L. Rough

Copyright 1987

The National Association of
Secondary School Principals
1904 Association Drive
Reston, Va. 22091
(703) 860-0200

ISBN 0-88210-195-1

Foreword

This book was written for students who wish to enhance their leadership potential and skills. We hope it will be read by a wide variety of students—those who have already assumed leadership roles and who may never have thought of themselves as leaders. This book is not only a manual for leaders, but also a call to leadership, a challenge for students to use and develop their skills and abilities to serve and lead others.

We wish to thank three people for their cooperation and help with the book. Janice Burkepile, our secretary, who spent many long hours at the word processor, and our spouses, Bev and Jim, for their love, support, and understanding.

John W. Gray
Angela Laird Pfeiffer

Contents

Chapter 5

COMMUNICATION SKILLS FOR LEADERS 41

Chapter 1

The Challenge of Leadership

To live is to risk.
To risk is to take action.
To take action is to lead.

In 1984, Bob Geldoff had an idea that seemed impossible. He wanted to organize a group composed of top British rock and roll artists to combine their talents toward solving the problem of world hunger. Geldoff also wanted to get record companies, producers, artists, and stores to donate all profits to the cause.

This "impossible" idea resulted in the recording of "Do They Know It's Christmas Time?" by Band Aid. This single song raised millions of dollars to fight hunger in Ethiopia and worldwide.

Harry Belafonte initiated a similar all-star effort called "USA for Africa." In less than a year this group, coordinated by Quincy Jones, Michael Jackson, and Lionel Richie, raised more than $200 million for worldwide famine relief through their concerts and album containing the hit single "We Are the World."

These efforts all originated with one man's vision. Bob Geldoff had an idea, and beyond that, he had both the determination to overcome obstacles, and the ability to motivate and coordinate others by making them believe in his ideas.

In short, Bob Geldoff is a contemporary example of leadership. He had the ability to see a need and the compulsion to do something about it, rather than sitting back and waiting for someone else to do something. He was able to convince others that they could contribute, then he coordinated the process of bringing all those people together.

Leadership is not, however, a phenomenon restricted only to adults and millionaire rock stars.

Several years ago, some Massachusetts high school students were distraught when several of their classmates were killed in an accident

1

caused by the teenage driver's drunkenness. They studied and learned the alarming national statistics regarding drunk driving. A study in Iowa, for example, showed that 50 percent of high school students are regular drinkers, and 32 percent drink heavily at least once a week. The American Red Cross revealed that one in three high school students rides in a car driven by a heavy drinker at least once a month, and 23 percent of high school students drink and drive.

The students in Massachusetts decided to do something. They formed "Students Against Drunk Driving" (SADD), which has now become a national organization dedicated to encouraging understanding between teenagers and their parents about drinking and driving.

Perhaps the major contribution of SADD has been a contract, which has now been signed by millions of teenagers and their parents nationwide. By signing the contract, a teenager pledges that he or she will not drive after drinking and will not get into a car with a driver who has been drinking. Instead, the teenager will call his or her parents for a ride. On their part, parents agree not to punish or lecture the teenager who is responsible enough to call and seek help. Any discussion of the matter will be done the next day, and will be supportive and controlled.

A Definition of Leadership

Writers have offered many different definitions of leadership. For the purposes of this book, leadership is defined as *taking the initiative to marshal resources toward end results.* Let's analyze this definition step by step.

● *Initiative.*

Leaders must have ideas and start people moving. Peters and Waterman in their book *In Search of Excellence*[1] noted that most successful managers have a "bias for action." These leaders consider the impact of their actions, yet they don't spin their wheels. They *do* something. They are decisive and willing to take calculated risks, without having *all* the answers beforehand. Leaders must be perceptive enough to notice a need, and take the lead to get people and resources together to meet the need.

● *Marshaling Resources.*

Leaders don't have to have all the answers, nor all the abilities and talents necessary to meet an objective. They do, however, need the organizational ability to bring needed resources together. Some of

1. Thomas J. Peters and Robert H. Waterman, Jr. *In Search of Excellence* (New York: Harper and Row, 1982).

these resources are people. A leader must identify and gain the cooperation of people who can contribute something worthwhile to a project. Leaders must help these people see the importance of their contribution toward meeting a need.

Take the example of Bob Geldoff. He had to make people aware of the dire famine around the globe. He also had to make rock stars believe that they could do something about it. Many of the rock stars, although they were concerned, probably didn't believe they could do anything about the situation. Geldoff was able to convince them that they could use their own talents to meet the need by combined action.

Once a leader has gained the cooperation of others, he or she must have the organizational ability to get people to work together and to make sure they have the material resources they need to meet the objective. The leader, then, must supply the coordination so that all the individual parts come together as a unified whole.

- *Toward End Results.*

Effective leadership is oriented toward goals. Someone who can gather loyal followers through the use of a nice personality or charisma, but is not effective in using those followers to achieve anything, is not a leader by definition. Leadership, then, is not a personal characteristic, but rather a dynamic process that works toward goal achievement.

Leadership is taking the initiative to marshal resources toward end results. All parts of the definition are important in understanding the leadership process.

Myths About Leadership

Because leadership is often a vague concept, many misunderstandings have developed. Some common misunderstandings, or myths, about leadership include the following:

Myth #1—Only "popular" people are leaders.

High school students tend to equate leadership with the captain of the football team, the captain of the drill team, or the homecoming queen. Certainly leadership is involved in these roles, but many leadership activities are not this public or glamorous. Anyone who organizes people to meet a need is a leader. The average student who is concerned with the poor in the community, and organizes a drive to collect toys to distribute for Christmas, is a leader.

Myth #2—Leaders are chosen or elected.

The truth is that leaders are often self-selected. Two types of leadership may be distinguished. One type could be called designated or appointed leadership. In this type of leadership, a leader is appointed or elected prior to the group beginning the task. This type of leadership process may sometimes happen in school organizations.

A second type of leadership is emergent leadership. In this type, a leader emerges because he or she has the vision, capabilities, or desire for leadership. In other words, the leader emerges to meet the need. Often, even in organizations with an official "appointed" leader, another individual may actually fulfill many of the leadership functions if he or she is more suited to leadership within the group.

Myth #3—You must have a formal position to be a leader.

This myth is closely associated with the first two. We may think that only the person elected to some formal office may exercise leadership within a group. However, an article by French and Raven called "A Formal Theory of Social Power," outlined five types of power that individuals may possess.[2]

1) *Legitimate power* is power that an individual has because of the formal position he or she holds. For example, a person may hold power because he or she is senior class president and president of the student council.

2) *Expert power* is a force that one has because he or she has special information, knowledge, or skills that are useful to a group. Perhaps someone that has expertise in computers, for example, might gain leadership in a project that requires such special knowledge.

3) *Coercive power* is the ability to force someone to do something, because of physical strength or damaging evidence.

4) *Reward power* is based on the ability to reward or punish someone for doing or refusing to do what you want.

5) *Referent power* is the influence you have over others because they identify with you as a person. In other words, they follow you because of your personal characteristics.

We see then that leaders may have power or influence for any number of reasons. Some leaders combine more than one of these. Yet one can be a leader without having a formal position, or legitimate power, as long as he or she has other bases of influence, such as knowledge or expertise.

Myth #4—You must be a great motivator of other people to be a good leader.

This myth has an element of truth in that a good leader must cer-

2. B.H. Raven and J.R.P. French, Jr. "A Formal Theory of Social Power." *Psychological Review* 63 (1956): 181-194.

tainly understand motivation. Yet motivation is not really something that one person can do for or to another. You cannot make someone be motivated. Yet a leader can understand and work with motivations. If, for example, a student's primary motivation is to be liked and admired by classmates, then the leader may be able to use that to encourage participation in a class project—"Help me to achieve this project, and you will help your classmates achieve their goal."

Myth #5—A leader only represents the wishes of the people that he or she leads.

Most people become leaders because they understand and relate to the desires and needs of those they lead. A leader can, however, do more than merely reflect the attitudes and values of followers. A leader can also actually transform followers through education and persuasion. A good example of this type of leadership was Mahatma Ghandi of India. He rose to prominence at a time when the Indians were repressed by the English colonists who controlled the country. Many of those around him advocated a violent overthrow of the British, yet Ghandi refused to accept this as a solution. Instead he took the basic needs that the Indians had for self-determination, and showed them how they might better achieve those needs through nonviolent resistance. He helped his followers understand different values. This type of leadership is called transformational leadership.

Myth #6—Males make better leaders than females.

It is interesting to note that most groups, even those that have a majority of women, choose a male for a leadership position. This probably reflects the fact that when we think of a leader we think of characteristics such as decisiveness, authority, and power, which are stereotypical male characteristics. But ideas about leadership are changing along with changing ideas about women.

We now recognize that women do exercise decisiveness and authority. Studies done recently analyzing male and female leaders have shown that there is little difference in their leadership styles, and the groups they lead are equally satisfied with male and female leaders. In addition, we now recognize that effective leaders must be decisive and authoritative, yet they must also be sensitive to the needs of the groups they lead and be comfortable with feelings. Sensitivity and emotion are stereotypically feminine characteristics. Thus, the most effective leadership combines what is thought of as male and female qualities. Warren Bennis, a business expert at the University of Southern California, has written that the most effective leadership style is androgynous, neither male nor female, but combining elements of both.

Myth #7—Leaders are born, not made.

This statement is most characteristic of the charismatic approach to leadership. Some people have said that certain individuals are born with traits that make them leaders—such as good looks, intelligence, or social prominence. Because they are so gifted, they will automatically become leaders in whatever field they choose. A person without these traits could not be an equally effective leader. Researchers for some time accepted this idea, and looked for "traits" that made some people leaders, and not others. Eventually, this research was fruitless because a standard list couldn't be formed. Leaders come from different backgrounds, have different skills and personalities, and become leaders for different reasons. Thus, the researchers concluded that leadership is less a "trait" than a "state." In other words, leadership is a process in which an individual emerges to meet a need. The person who takes the initiative in the situation is not a "great man," but often an ordinary person who rises to meet the challenge.

Leadership requires awareness and skills, which is something anyone can develop.

Challenges of Leadership

We have in the United States a strong demand for effective leaders to solve social problems. We especially need strong leaders in local communities and organizations. Yet too often apathy takes over, and we all wait for someone else to take charge.

Within your own school, a number of challenges cry out for effective leadership. Many organizations, from student government to the Future Farmers of America, need strong leadership. These organizations need people who can conduct meetings, increase group cohesiveness, and make the groups productive toward meeting goals.

Beyond the leadership needs of organizations, however, are the pressing social needs that face all teenagers. Suicide, for example, is now the leading cause of death among adolescents. With increasing pressures on young people, more and more teens are finding that they cannot cope. Too many of the programs formed to meet this problem are administered and led by adults. These adults may not understand or help as well as teenagers could. A student leader could take the initiative to develop programs that would meet the needs of fellow teens.

Another example of a social need is programs to combat drug and alcohol abuse. Teenage alcoholism and drug abuse are at an all-time high. Some teenagers have formed what they call "positive peer pressure groups" to provide information and positive support to other teenagers in their decisions about using drugs and alcohol. Funding for the peer programs to support advertising and educational programs are available from federal agencies. Again, this is an area of challenge for leadership.

A final example is poverty and hunger. Too often we isolate ourselves from acknowledging that hunger and poverty exist in our own communities. It is even easier to shirk the social responsibility of doing something about those less fortunate. We need young people, and people from all age groups, to see a need, and to organize individuals who could make a difference.

The challenges are clear and present. What is often missing is the vision, caring, and initiative of a leader to face and address the problems, and to marshal resources toward solving the problems.

Costs of Leadership

Leadership isn't always a positive and rewarding experience. Any time an individual takes a risk to defend a position or tries something new, there will be criticism. Some people always find it easier to criticize the actions of others than to take risks themselves.

Sometimes making others aware of a need requires "shaking them up" a little. It's more comfortable for some people to "wear rose-colored glasses," and to believe that problems are exaggerations that don't affect them directly. Take, for example, parents who refuse to believe that their children could ever be involved with drugs. Before you can get them involved and working toward a solution, you must disturb their complacency and make them realize that there is a problem which could easily involve their own children. They may be resistant at first to these efforts.

Leadership, therefore, is not always easy and leaders are not always popular. They often have to question commonly accepted beliefs, and challenge traditions that are wrong. In these efforts, leaders will always face resistance. Overcoming resistance is part of leadership.

Finally, leadership usually involves sacrifice. At the very least, one must sacrifice a great deal of time to serve in a leadership role. Coordinating the actions of others is time-consuming and often thankless. Leaders often sacrifice what they would like to do, or how they would like to do it, for the good and cohesiveness of the group.

Rewards of Leadership

Despite the costs of leadership, it is a rewarding activity. Leadership takes us out of selfish concerns to identify with something larger than ourselves. When we accomplish a goal, we experience a satisfaction that counts for something. It gives significance to our lives.

It's ironic that leadership almost always involves service. In order to lead, we must place our own importance and concerns below others. We must deny ourselves to help others. This idealistic approach to leadership is best summed up by the words of Theodore Roosevelt in 1910:

> *It is not the critic who counts; not the man who points out how the strong man stumbles, or where the doer of deeds could have done them better. The credit belongs to the man who is actually in the arena, whose face is marred by dust and sweat and blood; who strives valiantly; who errs, and comes short again and again; because there is not effort without error and shortcoming; but who does actually strive to do the deeds; who knows the great enthusiasms, the great devotions; who spends himself in a worthy cause, who at the best knows in the end the triumphs of high achievement and who at the worst, if he fails, at least fails while daring greatly, so that his place shall never be with those cold and timid souls who know neither victory nor defeat.*

Chapter 2

Understanding Communication

To lead is to communicate.
To communicate is to relate.
To relate is to share ourselves with others.

Friday afternoon has finally arrived and you've nearly survived another week of school. As you sit quietly, daydreaming about the weekend, the bell startles you. At the same moment the president of the student council waves to you from across the classroom and says, "See you at eight!"

You jump to your feet, gather your books, and follow the rushing crowd into the hall. As you move along a male voice from behind you says, "Ten days isn't enough, is it?" You have no idea what he's talking about, but you nod in agreement as the crowd pushes you away from the voice. After placing a few books in your locker you move out the door of the school into the warm afternoon sunshine.

The description above isn't an unusual set of events for a typical high school student. As a matter of fact, many readers may find themselves identifying with this person. Every day a set of similar events happens to each of us. Let's take a second look at this student's experiences and identify a few of the happenings that we might call communication events.

The act of daydreaming is common to all of us. This is intrapersonal communication or communication with the self. This behavior can be triggered by almost anything: a word, a sound, a sight, a smell. Our minds are ready at any moment to be carried off remembering the past or pondering the future. This intrapersonal communication is valuable because it helps us to avoid past mistakes and plan for the future. On the other hand, casual daydreaming can be a barrier to communication. Without intending to, we may be lost in our thoughts

9

at the very time when we should be actively listening, speaking, reading, or reacting. The sound of the bell jarred this student from his thoughts; the chain of events that followed, and the student's interpretation of them, were directly related to his daydreaming.

When the student council president called to him, our daydreamer wasn't in complete control of his senses and was in the process of going from daydreaming to reality. The words "at eight" may have been lost or misinterpreted. It's difficult to remember details when we're surprised, startled, or frightened. The message might have been received as "Don't be late!" "Can you skate?" or "Get a date!"

It's staggering to realize how often we misunderstand people because our minds are elsewhere. The fault is often with the daydreamer but just as often with the speaker. We blurt, yell, mumble, and toss our messages so carelessly that it's no surprise we're often misunderstood. Often we're so careless the listener is forced into daydreaming as his only avenue of escape.

The student in our description was puzzled by the remark, "Ten days isn't enough, is it?" This may have been a reference to a portion of the teacher's lecture, missed by the daydreamer as he was absorbed in his own thoughts. It may have been a time deadline for the next class assignment, also missed by the daydreamer. Or, if the student had been in complete control of his senses and not dazed, rushed, or pushed, he might have remembered a previous conversation which would make sense of the remark.

Let's look for a moment at the communication that took place outside the verbal statements. The bell communicated rather dramatically that the class was at an end. It was the bell above all else that contributed to the chain of events that followed. If the student moved slowly from his thoughts to the realities of the classroom, he might have made the transition in time to be aware of the sense and details of what followed.

The recognition of the first speaker as the student council president was another nonverbal event. Above all else (the message, the appearance, and the voice) the student recognized the speaker by his social and official position and title. The nonverbal message surrounds and sends the verbal message, and often the nonverbal will act as such a dramatic or impressive package that we ignore the verbal message. Many of us have heard the expression "What you are is speaking so loudly I can't hear what you're saying."

The student's jump to his feet and hurried exit from the classroom was prompted not only by the bell but by the crowd of classmates as they rushed out of the room. If there had been no communication of a need to hurry, the student might have sat quietly for a few seconds and recovered his senses before leaving the room. But people do not like to think the crowd is leaving them behind, and few want to offer evidence of having been daydreaming.

There are many more communication events, verbal and nonverbal, in the preceding passage; but the point has been made that a great portion of our day-to-day routine is associated directly with communication.

Communication as a Process

In general terms communication is a social event. Its function is to enable people to be with one another and to work well together.

Communication is a critical skill for leaders. It can be a direct avenue to reducing tensions and eliminating uncontrollable problems. Although we can do little to stop earthquakes and tornadoes, we can do something about many of our social problems such as racial discrimination, corruption in government, or neglect of the aging.

Communication provides us with the basic tools we need to make contact with each other and to work toward achieving day-to-day goals.

In fact, we spend most of our waking hours in some type of communicative act. From the moment we arise in the morning, we begin to communicate with our environment. Our alarm clock tells us it's time to get up, the sun rays coming through the window tell us what type of weather to expect, our body functions tell us if we're in good health. We are almost immediately greeted by some fellow human who starts the daily ritual of speaking and listening.

Most of the acts of communication are performed without much thought. We are creatures of habit, and one of our major habits is our daily communication ritual. We are so familiar with our communication habits that the process seems easy and simple. But that is not the case. It is a complex interaction of habits, attitudes, knowledge, information, and biases that we use in receiving and sending our messages to each other. What we say, how we say it, and how we react to what others say is all determined by our own complex communication system.

What actually happens when we communicate? In order to answer this question we must first recognize that communication is a process. It is a dynamic cycle of interpersonal influence. Figure 1 demonstrates this cycle.

We, as a source, decide to send a message. We compose the message by placing our idea into words. We then choose a channel through which we wish to send our message. For example, we may choose the oral channel (speech), the written channel (letters, memos, or notes), the visual channel (gestures, postures, or pictures), or perhaps a combination of several channels. Your message is sent through this channel to a second person who becomes the receiver. The receiver then interprets the message in terms of his or her own background and conditioning. In other words, the receiver sees and hears what he or she has been conditioned and trained to see and hear. The receiver then responds to these interpretations and gives meaning to your message. The meaning given will be the receiver's meaning and may or may not be the meaning you intended. For this reason senders of messages must work at being as clear and accurate as possible. We must also seek dialogue (continued communication back and forth) in order to ensure that our messages are getting through and that we are accurately receiving the messages of the other person.

Figure 1

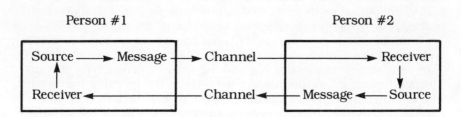

In this communication cycle both persons act as source and receiver. Each receives the feedback from the other and responds with his own message. The success of this communication is determined by:

(1) The source's ability to compose a message, to choose an appropriate channel through which to send it, and to interpret accurately the feedback message when the receiver responds; and

(2) The receiver's ability to receive accurately the source's message, compose a feedback message, and choose an appropriate channel.

This is obviously an oversimplification of the cycle but it does emphasize the continuous process we go through in communicating.

We take part in communicative cycles whether we choose to or not. It's impossible to avoid communicating. Keep in mind that we may not be communicating what we intend to communicate but we are communicating something.

Often our messages are misinterpreted. In those moments when we consider ourselves "neutral" or "uninvolved" our behavior is, nevertheless, being interpreted. When we are silent someone may interpret this as apathy or indifference. When we are undecided someone may interpret our actions as uncertain, doubtful, or fearful. We consciously or unconsciously communicate various attitudes and ideas throughout each day of our lives.

Myths About Communication

Two myths about communication should be exposed. Many people think, for instance, that *when they speak to someone, they have been understood.* Actually, meaning cannot be transmitted. It can only be stimulated or aroused in the receiver. The receiver must be an active participant for the cycle of communication to be complete.

Receivers translate messages into something familiar to their thinking. The translation is usually similar but it could be different from the way the source intended.

When a message is sent, the sender must attempt to stimulate or arouse meanings. The most common way of doing this is through the use of language (spoken, written, or by way of gesture).

The words of a language are symbols and don't have meanings. Only people have meanings, which may differ from person to person.

A word symbol always brings to the receiver's mind more than a dictionary definition. Take the word "block," for instance. What does the word mean? What does it bring to mind? If you heard, "My house is 16 blocks from school," would you know exactly how far that is? Much would depend on your concept of the length of a block.

Another confusion of meanings derived from words comes from context. Actually, the word "block" stimulates no real meaning alone, but must be put into a context before it acquires meaning. "A chip off the old block"; "the child's building blocks"; "the football player threw a good block"; or "the building is made of concrete blocks"; all give different meanings to the word "block."

A good deal also depends on how the receiver feels about the word he hears. If you are having problems with a contractor who is building your new home over the types of concrete blocks he is using, then you may have a negative reaction to hearing the word "block" in any context.

Words are symbols and are simply convenient for speaking of something in its absence or speaking of an abstract idea. Words are neither moral nor immoral, right or wrong. They are merely a system of stimuli we use to retrieve information stored in our brains. This retrieval system works well as long as we realize that one word may retrieve one thing from your brain and quite another from someone else's.

The meanings we have for words are restricted to the knowledge and experience we can bring to bear on them. So, as you transmit messages keep in mind that you're not transferring meaning, but sending selected stimuli to arouse meanings similar to your own.

The second myth about communication is that our eyes and ears tell us the truth. Although this may seem evident, there are many people who believe that everyone hears and sees the same thing in the same situation.

Have you ever heard three or four people describe the same football game or senior prom? The person's involvement in the event, past experiences with football games or proms, and ability to use the language all contribute to his or her description of the event.

A person's description of a past event often reveals more about the person than the event. What we choose to talk about and how we describe it reveals how we perceive things.

If we can accept the theory that all meanings exist in people, then the value of knowing your listener becomes evident. It is critical in good communication for each person to attempt to understand the ideas and attitudes from the other person's point of view. To understand and communicate with another is to know how it feels to speak as he or she speaks.

We can define communication in many ways. One of the broadest definitions calls it any "information-sharing activity."

For our purposes we shall restrict the definition to interpersonal communication (people to people). In this context we can define communication as "A process involving the organizing and sending of symbols in such a way as to help the receiver create in his own mind the meanings intended by the source." This means that communication is an attitude or mental condition that exists between people.

When we communicate we try to establish a common ground that assists the sender and receiver (the roles are interchangeable) in "tuning each other in." In order to be an efficient communicator we must develop our powers of empathy and concern for our receivers.

There is no better way to gain the receiver's ear and hold his attention than to express through our messages a concern for his welfare and a knowledge of his condition. This is not an easy thing to do. It requires time and patience, much more of both than we are usually willing to give.

Developing Communication Skills

If communication is an attempt to reach out to others and develop common ground, then how do we develop our abilities in this area? Communicating is not just a matter of saying something. It is not just a matter of luck. It requires skills. These skills do not magically appear when you become an adult. They are developed over a lifetime and your years in school provide an excellent training period.

You may wish to take advantage of opportunities to speak publicly, write, lead groups, engage in one-to-one dialogue, or debate. You will never learn until you take the risks involved in these opportunities. You may not always succeed, few of us do. Each experience, however, will add to your maturity as a communicator. Suggestions for developing skills as a communicator/leader are offered in the final chapter.

Communication as Relationship

Besides the basic social and language skills necessary in the acts of communicating, there is one basic concept that we must all understand. Any success we have in living is based directly on the quality of our relationships with other persons. Any special event or act that ends in good communication between two people began when one person turned to the other and accepted that person. Each person then built from his or her individual and private experiences outward to a frame of reference they could share.

We might say that fundamentally, communication is a relationship. When we successfully relate to others, we have successfully communicated with them. John Powell, a Jesuit psychologist, put it in these terms: "What I am, at any given moment in the process of my becoming a person, will be determined by my relationships with those who love me or refuse to love me, with those I love or refuse to love."[1] We are created by our relationships and we view our world through them.

Accepting this fundamental concept of communication does not make communication just one more of the busy things we do in life. Instead it becomes the basis for all our actions. It becomes our first thought when we take on the responsibilities of a leader. If we relate well to our audiences as speakers, to our readers or writers, and to our groups as chairpersons, we will have made the most important step toward effective leadership.

There are three basic social functions that communication serves for the leader:

1. It helps us discover who we are.
2. It helps us present ourselves to others.
3. It improves our social relationships and helps us contribute to our society.

We find out who we are by communicating with others. We feel important when we are listened to and valued for our opinions. Others tell us how we look, act, and sound. We bounce ourselves off of them and learn from the feedback.

If we are thoughtful and mature with our reactions to this feedback, we can develop accurate images of ourselves. If we are immature and overly sensitive to praise or criticism, we can develop false and damaging images of ourselves. But without others, we cannot know ourselves.

Communication also helps us to present ourselves to others. Through our words, gestures, and behavior, we paint a picture of ourselves. If we wish to be accepted as a leader, we must present an

1. John Powell, *Why Am I Afraid To Tell You Who I Am?* (Chicago, Ill.: Argus Communications, 1969), p. 43.

image that is trustworthy, able, and caring. If we wish to maintain this image, we must then live up to it and become this caring person.

We know that we must associate with people successfully to achieve our goals in life. The more we use our communication skills to assist our society in solving its problems, the more we ensure our own future. Our knowledge of communication will give us the ability to achieve certain task-related goals important to us, our families, and our society.

One of the major contributions communication can make in the development of a leader is to provide *credibility*. Credibility is based on judgments others make of you. These judgments are based on four aspects of your image: competence, trustworthiness, strength, and rapport.

You are judged as competent when you appear to be informed, experienced, and qualified. You are considered trustworthy if you seem fair, reliable, honorable, and honest. You are considered strong if you present yourself as bold, dynamic, assertive, and active. You are considered to have rapport if you are perceived as empathic, understanding, and sharing of other people's ideas and values.

The first step in gaining this credibility is to strive to achieve the personal attributes listed above. The second step is to use your communication skills to present yourself accurately and effectively to others. The third step is to make yourself aware of how others present themselves to you. This means that we must be willing to make ourselves available to others and listen as they present themselves to us. This is communication!

Chapter 3

Understanding Followers

To lead is to be in touch.
To be in touch is to give of yourself.
To give of yourself is to experience others.

If you are a leader, you are a people person. You reach your goals by dealing with groups of people. You depend on their cooperation and collective efforts to solve problems. With their help, you are able to accomplish larger tasks in a shorter period of time.

Your student council can do more for the student body and to solve school problems than you can alone. In the same way, your local school board can exert more power and influence than any one individual member of the board working alone.

A leader must understand "followers." Why do people join groups? How do group goals differ from individual goals? What are the group types? What are the strengths and weaknesses of groups? Answers to these questions will give the leader a better understanding of who follows a leader and why.

Why People Join Groups

People join groups to satisfy a need. Some needs may include recognition, money, social contacts, power, or entertainment.

Although the personal reasons for joining groups may vary significantly, members of a group usually recognize a common goal for the organization. They believe the group serves a purpose. Usually, members will stay as long as the group purpose and member's personal needs are being met. Good leaders will find ways to stay in contact with members' attitudes and motivation.

Group Purposes

The group purpose is significant to the leader. There are two general group purposes: social and task. The social group exists primarily to provide interaction among members and to develop relationships. Fraternities, bridge clubs, civic clubs, dinner clubs, country clubs, and garden clubs are examples of social clubs. These people gather for reasons such as similar interest, physical attraction, convenience of location, and the chance to meet people for social and professional purposes. If these individuals do not receive some personal satisfaction they would probably resign. The social group, then, is basically for the enjoyment of shared activities. If a leader recognizes the self-indulgent nature of these as necessary for social interaction, the job of leading the group will be easier.

The task group, on the other hand, is formed in response to some task that must be done. These groups can be found in business and industry where certain ongoing tasks must be accomplished. If members pool their energy, knowledge, and talents, the job is made easier and accomplished faster. They may be tackling a problem, designing a machine, or planning for the future. In any case, their tasks are operational and their attention is focused on accomplishment.

Other task groups help their members accomplish something personal. Examples would be therapy groups, weight-loss groups, educational groups, and exercise groups. Many of these would, of course, spend some time on social relationships but they remain task oriented.

Task groups share responsibilities among their members, elect leaders, and promote their operational goals. The U. S. Congress is such a group, as is the local high school student council. Leaders of these groups must be devoted to the group task and be able to solve problems and communicate effectively.

Group Behavior

As time passes, groups develop rules governing member behavior. What you can say, how you can say it, and when you can say it are norms that exist in groups. There are often norms regarding what you wear and how you behave. It may be proper to wear cut-off jeans and a sleeveless shirt to a fraternity meeting, but it may not be proper dress for church or a business conference. You may feel comfortable in leotards or shorts at your exercise class but uncomfortable if, after the class, you are going to a nice restaurant for dinner. These become obvious norms and are easily understood and accepted.

The norms become subtle when they involve such things as the amount of time you are expected to conduct serious work. Most new members of a group will observe the behavior of experienced members to learn appropriate actions. These groups expect members to conform to most or all of their norms.

Some behaviors affecting groups are related to self-concept. Members of a group decide who they are, which affects how they relate to other members. If you decide that you are intelligent, you make efforts to act intelligently and you expect to be treated as an intelligent person. If you feel that someone is "talking down to you," you are probably insulted. Your future interactions with that person will be affected by the event. Incidents such as this create defensive behavior and shape the group experience. If these incidents multiply, group cohesiveness is reduced.

A healthy respect for each other's self-concept is essential for the growth and development of groups. Finding ways to assist members in realizing their potential and in recognizing the potential and worth of other members is a major responsibility of the leader. This can be done by emphasizing group interdependence, stressing group goals, encouraging active participation, providing a supportive atmosphere, and developing group pride. The cohesiveness created by this type of leadership makes the group attractive to its members. This, in turn, will end in loyalty to the group and, in most cases, a productive organization.

As we watch individuals in a group, we observe various behaviors. Some talk often, others seldom talk. Some laugh, others never laugh. Some listen carefully, others seldom listen. If we could read their minds we would notice what is known as "hidden agendas."

These hidden agendas account for variety in behavior and are based on the personal needs of the individual members. The talkers may be attempting to gain control. The laughers may need acceptance. The silent ones may feel uninformed. Each has a private source of motivation that surfaces only in the context of accepted norms of the group. Leaders must understand that what happens on the task level may often be explained by what happens on the relationship level.

Relational Needs

In his book *The Interpersonal Underworld*,[1] William Schutz cites three interpersonal needs that act as a basis for our behavior as we relate to other people. These three needs are inclusion, control, and affection.

We all feel the need to be an individual even as we participate in groups. A member with a high need for inclusion seeks the attention of others. In its extreme, this may take the form of overt hostility, loud talking, dominating a conversation, or clowning. In moderate form, the behavior may be seen in such things as running for office, making

1. William Schutz, *The Interpersonal Underworld* (Palo Alto, Calif.: Science and Behavior Books, 1966).

motions, volunteering for tasks, or socializing with the current leaders. But, of course, not all members desire this much attention. If they have not felt successful in a group, they chalk it up to fate and decide there is no need to seek further attention. For most members the need for inclusion varies with the situation. They may seek recognition among friends in an informal group and shun attention when more formal groups ask for participation. The student council may have no success in getting them to run for office, but the cheerleader squad may find no resistance in naming such a person captain.

A group of people with high inclusion levels may find it difficult to conduct business with so many members seeking attention. On the other hand, a group of people with low inclusion needs may suffer a lack of leadership and participation. The group with a combination of both types probably functions best.

People also vary in the amount of control they need. Many of those who seek inclusion only want the recognition and do not desire power or control over the organization. Others need the control and power whether or not it ends in recognition. They are satisfied to be a behind-the-scenes leader as long as they influence the outcome. It is not wise for a leader to judge too quickly which members fall into which category. Both types are capable of making unique contributions to the group. It may be wise, however, for leaders to take an inventory of their own control needs. A good balance here provides more democratic and productive leaderships traits.

We all need affection. There are times when we need to be open and personal with our interactions. This behavior may or may not be appropriate for the norms of a group. A family group, a group of longtime friends, or a therapy group may have norms that not only allow this behavior but encourage it. Persons who have a high need for affection may be considered too friendly or personal if they seek to fulfill the need in inappropriate ways or places. If there are people present in a group who have low needs for affection they may be offended by overt displays of affection by others. It is more productive if the members of a group are sensitive to affection needs and respect the group norms. If a member does not like to become too familiar too rapidly this should be recognized and respected. These people may not seem compatible but generally they work together if there is mutual respect. A sensitive leader will be aware of this and assist in setting norms comfortable to all members.

Advantages of Groups

There are four major advantages to joining groups. They encourage meaningful relationships, assist us in learning problem-solving techniques, motivate us to develop commitments, and give us the advantage of numbers.

Groups not only give us reasons to be with others, they also encourage interaction. We often would not be in contact with certain individuals if we were not thrown together with them in organized groups. It would be difficult to maintain contacts with people of similar interests, talents, and purposes without the help of groups.

Once in a group, we have opportunities to observe the behavior of others and adjust our behavior accordingly. This learning experience speeds our social education and contributes to the development of our self-concept. By interacting with others we can present ourselves as we wish, and see how others think of us. Then, through this exchange of impressions, we form a self-concept that provides a set of roles that we are forced to or choose to play. Supportive and cohesive climates in groups give us a better chance at developing a healthy self-concept.

In most circumstances, groups arrive at better decisions than individuals working alone. This is especially true when the goal is to achieve a quick and correct answer. A technical problem that requires factual data is more easily handled by a group. Facts can be gathered and solutions offered in greater number by a group. The interaction contributes to solid decisions as members ask questions and share ideas.

Members who experience group identity feel a loyalty to the group. They learn the value and satisfaction of commitment. This, in turn, will contribute direction and purpose to an individual member's life. For instance, a member of a high school student council may become a loyal supporter of colleagues on the council and may feel committed to representing the student body's needs. This training in commitment may be positive enough to persuade the person that this valuable experience can be repeated. So, upon graduation, the person enters politics, is elected to office, and is highly successful as a loyal representative of his or her constituents. It becomes a satisfying and rewarding way of life.

The final and obvious advantage of groups is numbers. There is often an advantage to having the help of a large membership. They can influence people of authority, pool resources for greater advantage, and reward with symbols of status. The group can even take blame and absorb expense more readily than individuals. For this reason, people often like to "hide" in an organization since they feel inadequate alone.

Disadvantages of Groups

Groups are not always more effective than individuals. They do have limitations. Often a group does not possess the collective expertise of one individual. The group could be merely pooling its ignorance. Advice from such a group could never be considered as valuable as that of an expert. When groups fail to take advantage of individual experts they limit their options and ignore available sources of information. This expert opinion is often ignored because it doesn't support the group's current opinion. Often a leader can make a significant contribution to the group by insisting on, or at least encouraging, procedures that ensure the use of all available expertise.

There are other disadvantages of groups. Discussion, for example, requires time and some decisions require quick solutions. The time factor may be honored at the expense of minority opinion or through investigation. There are also member types that inhibit effective group action, including dominating personalities who force their opinions on groups, people who place status above democratic action, and the person who has little knowledge of group dynamics but insists on obstructing the process.

One of the very serious shortcomings of groups is associated with conformity. The early and simple forms of conformity such as adapting to norms and seeking consensus on issues are normal and expected. When this conformity becomes a mindless group operation that surrenders its code of beliefs, it can end in what is known as "groupthink." Psychologist Irving Janis says that groupthink is the desperate drive for consensus at any cost. In other words, it states that when we all think alike none of us may be thinking very much. A group operating under pressure for a long period of time and suffering from information overload, fatigue, and prejudice is a candidate for groupthink. Studies show that cohesive groups are highly vulnerable to this condition. The friendly and close relationships become part of a hidden agenda in these groups.

A high school senior honors English class contained many friends who had been together since junior high school. They all knew how important grades could be in securing college admission and financial aid. The teacher assigned difficult work and had rigorous standards for the class. The students became obsessed with studying together and encouraging each other's progress. Shortly after mid-term the teacher suggested that the students reduce the amount of study in English and apply more effort in math and other subjects. The students responded with, "How can anyone understand math, history, and science if they cannot read and write?" They continued their fanatic devotion to English studies. When SAT and ACT scores were released, only a fourth of the class had scores high enough for admission to the college of their choice. The determining factor was the low scores made in subjects outside English. The practical objective which began their studies, college admission scores, was lost in the group madness. Their addiction to only one course of action and resistance to the teacher's suggestions is typical of groupthink.

Researchers have only begun to study the phenomenon of groupthink. We aren't ready to give instruction on how to handle it, but we can offer one suggestion. If you are the leader of a cohesive group that finds itself under long-term pressure, you might try calling for a recess or helping the group consider new options and perspectives. This may seem a simple action but it is about as concrete a suggestion as we can offer at this time. Just knowing that groupthink exists may help you notice its symptoms and prevent it.

Whatever we can do to better understand people as they interact in groups will make us more responsive leaders. People are complex as individuals and this complexity multiplies as individuals combine in groups. As leaders, our job is to activate groups toward their goals. To do this we must understand our followers.

Chapter 4

Understanding Yourself as a Leader

To lead is to grow.
To grow is to seek truth.
To seek truth is to understand yourself.

.

Before leaders can really understand others, they must work toward a clear and realistic understanding of themselves. How we see ourselves affects the messages we send to others, and the way we interpret communication from others. Your effectiveness as a communicator-leader depends in no small degree upon your self-image, the extent to which others accept that image, and the interaction of your image of yourself and their image of you. We might think of the self-concept as a "screen" that we hold up in front of us. Our impressions of others, and their actions toward us, are all filtered through that screen. Often the screen can distort our perception. We have heard about the person "with a chip on his shoulder" who is ready to interpret every message negatively because he is angry at the world in general. We've also heard of the person who wears "rose-colored glasses" and who often sees things in an unrealistically positive way. Leaders must understand how their self-concept affects communication sent to and received from others.

Defining of Self-Concept

Our self-concept is the total of the things we feel we know about ourselves through our interaction with others. We characterize ourselves as: "a good organizer," "a shy person," "a devout Christian," "an athletic person," or "not that kind of girl." Certain group memberships, in a church, club, or team, may form a large part of our identities. Abilities, friends, families, and positions also contribute to how we view ourselves.

Many times we try to explain our "true" self to someone. Perhaps we try to explain some behavior with which we are not comfortable by saying, "I'm really not like that," or "That is not my true personality." In reality there is no "one true self" for anyone. All of us have many "true selves," and it is important for us to understand and accept all of them.

It is natural that we adapt to different people and situations by choosing behavior that is appropriate to that person and setting. The person who behaved the same at a football game and a church service probably would not fit in at least one of the settings. All of us have some people and settings with which we feel more and less comfortable.

Self-Fulfilling Prophecy

We also should realize that there is a close connection between how others see us and how we see ourselves. One way that these two images of self are related is a phenomenon called the "self-fulfilling prophecy." Often when we are repeatedly told that we have certain talents and capabilities, we believe those messages. We become outstanding because we know others expect it.

Less fortunately, sometimes we are given negative messages when we are young which affect our development adversely.

The best example of self-fulfilling prophecy is an experiment that occurred several years ago in two elementary classrooms. A teacher was given two classes, and was told that one class was an accelerated class of gifted learners. She was told that the other class was a class with learning disabilities. The students were capable of learning, but would be slow in their progress. The two classes were actually the opposite of what she had been told. By the end of the semester the slow learners had achieved remarkable progress, while the accelerated class had suffered declines in learning. The achievements of the classes were probably closely related to the teacher's expectations, which could have been communicated to the students in a variety of subtle ways.

This self-fulfilling prophecy can certainly be related to leadership. Some students may have been "raised" to be leaders. Their families and friends gave them confirming messages, and expected high standards of performance from them. These students might always hold the assumption, without even considering it, that they would lead others, and this prophecy in many cases does come true. On the other hand, other students may have avoided leadership roles because early in their lives they were given negative messages about their capabilities and promise. These students may feel that they have nothing to contribute because they know they are not expected to be leaders by those who are close to them.

It is important as we grow older that we begin to examine those early assumptions that we accepted without question as children. History is filled with examples of leaders who were practically written off by many people early in their lives, but who went on to achieve great things. Thomas Edison enrolled in school two years late because he had scarlet fever, which caused hearing impairment. He was judged by teachers to be stubborn, aloof, and backward. His I.Q., as measured by the schools, was low, and he alienated his family at a young age by burning down his father's barn. This great inventive talent might have been lost if Edison believed everything he was told about himself.

Albert Einstein was also judged to have a low I.Q. as a child. He was considered poorly adjusted, unsociable, and disruptive in school, frequently withdrawing into a fantasy world. He was often sick, and had a nervous breakdown that caused him to be removed from school. He had no real goals or objectives when he was young, yet went on to revolutionize the field of physics.

One more example illustrates how misleading early impressions can be. As a child Eleanor Roosevelt was described as unattractive and homely. She had a mediocre I.Q. She was sickly, bedridden, and often hospitalized. She wore a backbrace because of spinal defects. Her father was an alcoholic. She often daydreamed, or engaged in disruptive behavior to gain attention. Most of her elementary teachers would never have dreamed that she would go on to become one of the most respected First Ladies in the history of the United States.

The point is that what others think of us is important, and can shape us in many ways. If we grow up with positive messages and support, we have an edge in being able to see ourselves as leaders. We must, however, evaluate the messages we receive from others to see if we believe them as we grow older. Only then can we overcome those early negative impressions to achieve great leadership.

Self-Reflection

Not only do others' impressions often create how we see ourselves, as in the case of self-fulfilling prophecy, but also how we see ourselves can be influential in shaping how others see us. As a teacher in a speech communication classroom, I used to play a game with students. I would tape a message to each student's forehead. The messages said things like, "Disagree with everything I say," or "Don't take me seriously," or "Get angry with me," or "Agree with me." The students could not see the messages I had taped to their foreheads. I then asked them to talk to others in groups, and directed the students in the group to treat each student in the manner that the forehead note indicated. It didn't take long for the students to become restless because they couldn't understand why others were reacting to them in the way they were. The students would pull out mirrors, or try to look into windows to get a clue to the messages on their foreheads.

If you think about it, we all interact with notes on our foreheads. We send both verbal and nonverbal clues that tell them how we expect to be treated. If you look away from someone you're talking to and use a soft voice, you may be telling him that you fear him, or that you don't feel equal to him. If you talk to someone in an aggressive voice, you may be telling them to be defensive and to argue with you, even though you may not intend that. Just like the notes on the forehead, we are often unaware of these messages, which are quite clear to others. Others become a "mirror" that reflects back to us the impression we have of ourselves. Thus, if we do not like the reactions we are getting from others, the first step is to hold up a "mirror" and analyze our own behavior to see if messages we are sending might be bringing out these reactions in others.

Learning What Others Think

Even though we have demonstrated a close relationship between others' opinions and self-concept, it is often difficult to know exactly how we are seen by others. People don't usually come out directly and tell us how they see us. Therefore, we must often draw our conclusions from the way they act toward us. Keep in mind, however, that our conclusions may be biased by the view we already have of ourselves. If I have a low self-impression, I may see snubs or insults from others, even when that is not what they intend. If I have a high self-concept, I may ignore negative information that is not consistent with the way I view myself.

Some leaders think of themselves as successful because of their good ideas and magnetic personality when, in reality, they were chosen as leaders because they are good looking or athletic. These leaders' self-concept is a product of their own minds. Their image to the group may be one of "dumb beauty" or "popular jock," but still admired and respected by the group.

The leader's image and the images groups have of the leader may come in conflict and present serious communication problems. The best way to prevent this is to seek as honest and objective a self-concept as possible.

Striking a Balance

Even though it is important for leaders to have a realistic idea of how others see them, it is also important to strike a balance between their own self-image and the impressions of others. None of us, and especially not the leader, can live in this world and pretend not to care at all about what others think. We all depend on people too much. The leader must care. Without followers, he or she cannot be a leader.

Information is important, but we should keep it in perspective. I have seen students who lost an election, for example, who felt utterly destroyed, and who suddenly felt they had no worth or leadership potential. They were giving the impressions of others too much weight, and ignoring all the valuable qualities that they knew they had.

Ask yourself several questions in evaluating the feedback you receive.

1. How well do they know you? Casual comments from relative strangers may give us clues as to the first impressions we make on others, but may not give reliable information about more important elements of ourselves.
2. What does the feedback really mean? Often people in school elections may vote on little more than name recognition. Thus, a defeat in an election may mean that your name is not memorable, but may or may not mean anything beyond that.
3. Why does the other person draw that impression? Often we may send clues that lead people to false impressions about us. If we know *why* someone drew a certain conclusion, we will be in a better position to interpret that impression. Then we can modify our own behavior to create different impressions.

The Impact of Goals on Self-Concept

The goals we set for ourselves, and the way we achieve them, or fail to achieve them, have an important impact on how we see ourselves. Often we allow others to define our goals for us.

Sometimes parents have goals for their children. They decide on their careers, their colleges, or they seek certain standards of popularity. Parents may want the child to achieve all the same things that they or an older brother or sister did. Parents may also want the child to achieve all the things that they wanted to do, but didn't. Sometimes our friends set our goals for us, and define what is important or valuable to achieve.

If you accept goals from others that you do not genuinely and wholeheartedly want for yourself, then you will probably fail. If you strive to be a leader only because your family wants you to, or because your friends think it would be great, then you may not achieve success. Even more harmful, you may set up a cycle of failure. If you halfheartedly work toward a goal that was not yours to begin with, you fail. After a few failures you begin to develop a negative self-concept. Then you may fail because of your negative attitude. You begin to believe you cannot achieve anything.

29

Think about what you want to do and set reasonable, achievable goals. If you're unrealistic, you may create the same cycle of failure. On the other hand, progress toward goals, even small steps, can gradually build an attitude of achievement and self-worth.

Improving Self-Concept

If you feel dissatisfied with the way you currently see yourself, then you may want to work on a more positive self-concept.

● *Focus on the Positive.*

One way to improve self-concept is to focus on your positive qualities. How many times have you lain awake at night thinking of all the dumb and embarrassing things you did during a given day? Don't those impressions get worse as you dwell on them? How many times have you considered your positive qualities and the good things you have done? Probably not as often. Somehow in a quest for modesty, we are conditioned not to dwell on our positive characteristics. We feel uncomfortable with compliments when they are given. We squirm when we have to talk about ourselves, or say anything nice about ourselves to others. While it may be desirable to be modest, we should not focus only on the negative. We ought to feel more comfortable in noting and acknowledging our positive qualities, especially to ourselves.

● *Self-Disclosure.*

It is also helpful to be able to talk about yourself to other people. Often our problems and shortcomings seem more difficult to handle because we feel that we are the only people in the world who have the problem or feel that way.

When we are able to talk with others, we realize that we are not alone, and our situation is not unusual. In addition, self-disclosure often helps relationships.

Too often leaders feel that they must hide feelings of insecurity, anger, doubt, or fear because of their leadership positions. But we often assign even more credibility to someone who is secure enough to admit that they don't know something, or that they have doubts. When we see that a leader is human, we may identify with him or her even more because we feel something in common.

● *Focus Outwardly.*

A third suggestion for improving self-concept is to focus outwardly instead of inwardly on ourselves. People who remain completely self-absorbed, wondering what impression they are making on others, and worrying about looks and social standing are often less secure than those who are able to care more about others than themselves. Leadership can be a way to improve self-concept because you're involved with serving others, giving you little time to focus in an unhealthy way on yourself.

● *Unconditional Self-Respect.*

If you were asked to write down the times that you feel best about yourself, what would you write? If you're like most of us, you'd probably write things like, "When I make good grades," or "When I help someone else," or "When I achieve what I want to." All these answers indicate that our liking and respect of ourselves is based on performance.

If you have a week when you make a touchdown in the game, make an A on a test, or make the drill team, then you feel wonderful about yourself. However, if you fail at something that is important to you, then your feelings for yourself may hit rock bottom.

A fluctuation of self-concept based on things you do may be unhealthy because it isn't stable. A more sound basis for self-concept is unconditional self-respect. This simply means that *whatever* you do or don't do, you're entitled to a certain level of respect and liking for yourself simply because you're a human being. You're important and special simply because you're you.

If you accept this idea, then suddenly accomplishments become things that you do *because* you care about yourself, not *in order* to care about yourself. Accomplishments come much more easily when they come from a positive self-image, instead of as a desperate attempt to earn respect.

When you can accept yourself unconditionally, it's easier to accept others unconditionally. Mutual acceptance leads to more effective leadership, and allows you to show respect for all followers, even if they don't meet all of your expectations.

Work To Change, and Learn To Accept

The last suggestion to improve self-concept is to work to change the problems that are important to you and accept the things that you don't care about enough to change. We can all direct our lives and be what we want to be within the physical limitations we are born with. If a certain characteristic or trait is standing in the way of a more healthy self-concept, then change it. If you lose your temper too much, then make an action plan to develop more patience and control. Seek outside help if necessary. If you're overweight and hate yourself for it,

31

then lose the weight. It's difficult to make changes. It requires sacrifices and effort, but it can be done.

If you find yourself unwilling to make the sacrifices necessary to change yourself in a certain area, then chances are that it's not that important to you. If you want to lose weight, but you continue to eat in ways that don't allow the weight to come off, then obviously, at this time, eating is more important to you than losing weight. The pleasure of eating outweighs the pleasure of looking different. If it didn't, then you wouldn't make that decision. Accept the decision.

A more active lifestyle may be more important to you than time-consuming make-up or hair styles. You'd rather spend the time doing something else. Accept your decision.

Life is full of trade-offs and comparisons. The biggest thing is not to feel bad or guilty for something that you have decided not to do. If it becomes important enough to you, you will change it. Until then, accept yourself as you have decided to be.

Understanding Yourself as a Leader

Once you begin to understand yourself more as a person, you can begin to understand yourself as a leader. The first step is to look honestly and deeply within yourself to understand the reasons why you want to be a leader. There are no unacceptable motives, but you do need to understand them.

David McClelland of Harvard University says that we have three different needs as human beings. The first need is for power. We need to feel control over ourselves, and to some extent, over others. We need to feel that we can influence events and have importance in the big scheme of things.

A second need is for achievement. We need to feel that we are making progress and accomplishing things.

A final need is for affiliation. This means that we need social connections with others.

All of these human needs can be motivations for leadership. We may have needs in all three areas, but usually one need is somewhat predominant over the others. Some leaders are primarily motivated by control. They like to be in charge, directing the work of others. Other leaders may be motivated by achievement, by getting jobs done. They like to be in a leadership position because they can directly see their contributions to progress. Still other leaders are motivated by affiliation. They love to be in the center of a group of people, working with a variety of individuals. Their leadership position confirms that they are liked and needed by others.

Several conclusions about these motive profiles can be drawn. First, some interpersonal needs are more "natural" for leadership than others. Among the majority of leaders, motives of control or achievement are the most common.

Most leaders like the feeling of controlling a group, or of getting things done. Sometimes we are almost ashamed of our control motives, and try to mask them, or explain them away, but you should realize that if you experience a need for control, then you are like many other people drawn to leadership positions.

To be an effective leader, you must exercise responsible control, thus, it is only natural that you feel comfortable in a control position. It is only when the need for control is so extreme that the leader becomes insensitive to others that it is harmful.

A second conclusion is that you need some "match" of motive profiles with the people you lead. You cannot always assume that other people in your group are motivated by the same needs as you.

You may be motivated to do your best work by a sense of achievement. But someone else may be motivated by affiliation. It's easy to impose your motives on someone else and assume that if a person is laughing and joking around while working, he isn't really serious about achievement. However, that may be how the person does his best work. He is motivated when social needs are met during work.

Often, if the high school student body doesn't want to do what the leader thinks they ought to do, the student body is labeled as "apathetic." That may not be the case. It may be that they simply have different needs. Leaders must realize that they cannot just pour motivation into others, but must work with the motivation that people already have. They must make tasks fulfill the varied needs of followers.

A third conclusion about motives is that you can develop a stronger need in other areas simply by exercising them. Perhaps, for example, you are a leader with a primary need for control, but you find yourself leading a group with predominant needs for affiliation. You might modify your leadership style by increasing your own needs for affiliation. If you can be more social as a leader, you can better meet the needs of your group. That way you'll command more loyalty from the group because you are meeting their needs.

Another example might be that you became a leader because you are a social person and you love to be with other people. You're elected to a leadership position because you care about others. You find, however, that in your new role simply liking other people and enjoying their company isn't enough to be effective. Therefore, you should develop more of a need for control as well as affiliation. You should become more comfortable in exercising control over others.

Leadership Style

Your motivations for leadership can have a large influence over the style you adopt as a leader. One style of leadership is authoritarian.

The authoritarian leader exercises absolute control over the group. He or she must review every decision personally, and be involved in each task. The authoritarian leader usually has a high concern for task. He or she is most concerned with getting the job done and secondarily with people. An authoritarian leader might say, "People don't have to like me, but they must respect me," or "It's a difficult and thankless job, but someone's got to be sure the work gets done."

In the past, the authoritarian style was considered synonymous with leadership. Many people assumed that to be a leader, a person must be tough and unyielding. People wouldn't work unless they were watched over and guided. Recently, however, more people have realized that other leadership styles may also be effective, perhaps even more effective in most situations, than the authoritarian style.

Another style of leadership is democratic or participative. This style of leadership is also called team leadership. This style uses the members of the group as resources. The leader is concerned about accomplishing tasks, but is also concerned about the human needs of group members. The leader is more likely to delegate tasks and coordinate rather than to control actions.

To test your own leadership style, take the following short quiz:

Leadership Questionnaire

Directions: The following items describe aspects of leadership behavior. Respond to each item according to the way you would most likely act if you were the leader of a work group. Circle whether you would most likely behave in the described way: always (A); frequently (F); occasionally (O); seldom (S); or never (N).

A   F   O   S   N   1. I would most likely act as the spokes-man of the group.

A   F   O   S   N   2. I would encourage after-school and weekend work.

A   F   O   S   N   3. I would allow members complete freedom in their work.

A   F   O   S   N   4. I would encourage all members to follow the rules.

A   F   O   S   N   5. I would permit the members to use their own judgment in solving problems.

A   F   O   S   N   6. I would stress being ahead of competing groups.

A   F   O   S   N   7. I would speak as a representative of the group.

A   F   O   S   N   8. I would needle members for greater effort.

A   F   O   S   N   9. I would try out my ideas in the group.

A   F   O   S   N   10. I would let the members do their work the way they think best.

A   F   O   S   N   11. I would be working hard for personal recognition.

A   F   O   S   N   12. I would tolerate postponement and uncertainty.

A   F   O   S   N   13. I would speak for the group if there were visitors present.

A   F   O   S   N   14. I would keep the work moving at a rapid pace.

A   F   O   S   N   15. I would turn the members loose on a job and let them go to it.

A   F   O   S   N   16. I would settle conflicts when they occur in the group.

A   F   O   S   N   17. I would get swamped by details.

A   F   O   S   N   18. I would represent the group at outside meetings.

A   F   O   S   N   19. I would be reluctant to allow the members any freedom of action.

A   F   O   S   N   20. I would decide what should be done and how it should be done.

A   F   O   S   N   21. I would push for increased productivity in assigned tasks.

A   F   O   S   N   22. I would let some members have authority but only those members I felt I could control.

A   F   O   S   N   23. Things would usually turn out as I had predicted.

A   F   O   S   N   24. I would allow the group a high degree of initiative.

A	F	O	S	N	25. I would assign group members to particular tasks.
A	F	O	S	N	26. I would be willing to make changes.
A	F	O	S	N	27. I would ask the members to work harder.
A	F	O	S	N	28. I would trust the group members to exercise good judgment.
A	F	O	S	N	29. I would schedule the work to be done.
A	F	O	S	N	30. I would refuse to explain my actions.
A	F	O	S	N	31. I would persuade others that my ideas are to their advantage.
A	F	O	S	N	32. I would permit the group to set its own pace.
A	F	O	S	N	33. I would urge the group to beat its previous record.
A	F	O	S	N	34. I would act without consulting the group.
A	F	O	S	N	35. I would ask that group members follow standard rules and regulations.

If you frequently engage in behaviors 1, 2, 6, 8, 11, 13, 19, 20, 22, 23, 25, 29, 30, 34, and 35, you may tend toward an authoritarian style of leadership. You take control, and like things to be done your way.

The key to interpreting your own results is to look at the entire pattern of your answers. You might serve as a spokesman, for example, in some situations without being autocratic or authoritarian. However, if you find yourself falling into a pattern on several of the above questions, you may be an oppressive leader who isn't using the people you lead as effectively as you could.

On the other hand, if you frequently engage in behaviors 5, 9, 24, 26, 28, then you probably tend toward a team pattern of leadership, which is productive for the group and its members. You trust the members, and try to gain their best efforts by letting them exercise their own responsibility and creativity. You don't force your ideas on the group, but rather rely on the strength of group problem solving, using the combination of many good minds to bear on a problem.

Of course you should only use this quiz as a rough approximation of your leadership style. It's limited by your own objectivity in answering questions, and in the limited items tested. To get an even better idea of your leadership style, you should monitor your own behavior and consult others about their perceptions.

Blake and Mouton have described four patterns of leadership grid.[1] The grid is set up as a graph using two axes. One axis is concern for people, and the other is concern for task. Based on these two dimensions, we can isolate five different styles.

The Leadership Grid

High 9	1/9 (country club): Purpose is incidental to lack of conflict and good fellowship. Country club approach.	9/9 (team): Purpose is integration of requirements.
8		
7		
6		5/5 (middle of the road): Purpose comes first: but morale can't be ignored. Push enough to get the work, but give enough, too, to get morale necessary.
5		
4		
3		
2	1/1 (impoverished): Purpose is unobtainable because people are lazy and indifferent. Sound, mature relationships are difficult to achieve because conflict is inevitable.	9/1 (task): Men are commodity just as machines. A leader's responsibility is primarily to plan, direct, and control the work.
Low 1		

(y-axis label: Concern for People)

```
1    2    3    4    5    6    7    8    9
Low      Concern for Production      High
```

A 9/1 style of leadership (task) is typical of a leader who has a need for achievement and a low concern for people and how they feel about the job. This leader will often force people, or use manipulative strategies to get others to do what he wants done.

A 1/9 leadership style (country club leader) is a leader who is concerned about people, but has little concern for production. This type

---

1. Robert Blake and Jane Mouton, *The Managerial Grid* (Houston, Tex: Gulf Publishing Co., 1964).

of leader doesn't want to offend people, and will often do things himself to avoid causing inconvenience to others.

The 1/1 style of leadership (impoverished) is illustrated by leaders who aren't concerned about people or production. This type of leader avoids decisions, is neutral in conflicts, and maintains an atmosphere of apathy. Often this type of leader has been forced into a position without much enthusiasm for it, or is burned out from too much work and too little recognition or reward for it.

The 9/9 style (team) leadership is characterized by a concern for both people and production. They try to keep group cohesiveness while solving task productivity. They allow consensus in decision making, confront and resolve conflict, maintain an atmosphere of trust and acceptance, and encourage candid and spontaneous feedback from group members.

The 5/5 (middle of the road) style is exemplified by leaders who have a moderate concern for people and their productivity. Their philosophy is to be firm but fair. They negotiate conflict by seeking compromise. The result may be that followers think they are being manipulated rather than being trusted. Decision making is usually handled by majority rule unless the conflict is too great. In short, middle-of-the-road leaders seek the approval of others, but often lack the courage or strength to take unpopular positions that may be in the best long-term interests of the group.

Blake and Mouton stress that leaders should strive for the 9/9 style in which leaders work together with the groups they lead to achieve a great deal, but never lose sight of the people who make the production happen. It's difficult to balance concerns for getting the job done along with trying to pay attention to "people problems." Still, both are necessary and work together for the best outcome.

Ethics

The last topic, which is important for leaders to understand, is ethics. Ethics is vital to leadership, because we evaluate leaders not only on their accomplishments, but on their ethics.

If people were asked if Hitler or Nixon were great leaders, answers might be mixed. Certainly both men accomplished a great deal, and both were masters of persuasion and politics. Yet their leadership was tainted because of their ethical stances that the end justified the means.

Joseph DeVito, in his book on interpersonal communication, describes three different systems of ethics.[2] The first system is based

2. Joseph A. DeVito, *The Interpersonal Communication Book*, 3rd ed. (New York: Harper & Row, 1983) pp. 47-64.

on the writings of Karl Wallace,[3] and is based on the key values of a democratic society. On the basis of these values, Wallace suggests four "moralities," which he feels should guide communication in a free society:

1. A communicator in a free society must recognize that during the moments of his utterances he is the sole source of argument and information. This means that leaders should be well informed, and will not claim facts that she or he has not verified.
2. The communicator who respects the democratic way of life must select and present fact and opinion fairly. The leader must then present facts in a way that allows the follower choice in deciding among alternative positions.
3. The communicator who believes in the ultimate values of democracy will invariably reveal the sources of his information and opinion. Only by knowing the sources can the audience evaluate the information fairly.
4. A communicator in a democratic society will acknowledge and respect diversity of argument and opinion. You will respect even those who disagree with you.

A second system of ethics is based on the idea of freedom. According to this position on ethics, the leader must provide the greatest freedom of self-determination for each follower. Under this system, proposed by Paul Keller and Charles Brown, communication is ethical when there is acceptance of the responses of others, without trying to change or deny their freedom to feel as they want.[4]

A final system of ethics described by DeVito is one of ethical basis for choice. It's assumed that individuals have a right to make their own choices.

Interpersonal communication is ethical to the extent that it facilitates the individual's freedom of choice by presenting the other person with accurate bases for choice.

Communication is unethical to the extent that it interferes with the individual's freedom of choice by preventing the other person from getting information relevant to choice. For example, communication strategies, such as lying, manipulating with fear or emotional ap-

3. Karl Wallace, "An Ethical Basis of Communication," *Communication Education* 4 (1955): 1-9.
4. Paul W. Keller and Charles T. Brown, "An Interpersonal Ethic for Communication," *Journal of Communication* 18 (1968): 73-81.

peals, or forcing someone, are unethical because they don't allow informed choice.

When there is a question of ethics, you must decide if you believe that the ends justify the means. You must decide whether material things are more important in some instances than personal satisfaction. You must determine whether you feel that moral values are relative. All these decisions will deeply affect your leadership style, and the direction in which you lead others.

Chapter 5

Communication Skills for Leaders

To lead is to influence.
To influence is to change.
To change is to survive.

In preceding chapters we have discussed leadership, followership, and how both are related to interpersonal communication. This final chapter is devoted to a treatment of the personal, interpersonal, and social skills that are essential to good leadership. Practical suggestions are given for developing a variety of these communication skills.

This chapter is followed by a list of suggestions and exercises for your personal improvement and for developing the skills of your groups. You also may wish to consult the reading list at the end of this book for further resources.

Goal Setting

The ability to set goals is essential for personal or group achievement. Too often our goals are fuzzy and general. We may have a personal goal to be more disciplined, or we may have a group goal to be more productive. The problem with these goals is that they aren't specific enough to provide a meaningful target for action.

Good goals or objectives have four characteristics:

1) They are *specific*.

They do not deal in abstract qualities, but in specific behaviors. Thus, instead of stating that you will be more disciplined, a better goal statement might be, "I will get up at 7 in the morning," or "I will complete each day's homework on the day it's due."

2) They are *measurable*.

Your objective should be written in a way that one can observe your actions to see how well you have met your goals. For example, if you simply say you'll make better grades, then it's not clear what your real goal is. Even one point extra on one pop quiz is improving your grades, yet may not satisfy your real ambition. A better objective would be "I will raise my grade point average to 3.0 by my senior year." This objective is measurable, and has the standard of evaluation written into the objective.

3) A good objective is *achievable*.

Goals can actually hurt the motivation of an individual or a group if they are unrealistically high. The group or person may initially work hard, but as they see that their best efforts cannot meet the high standard, they may become discouraged and feel like failures, giving up on the goal.

4) A good goal is *challenging*.

While unrealistically high goals may hurt motivation, goals that are too easily met may also hurt best efforts. All of us need goals to work toward which demand from us our strongest effort and force us to improve ourselves.

As a leader, you may be careful to build group consensus on goals. The leader must be careful not to impose his or her goals on the group. Only when members fully identify with the group's goals will they commit their time and energy to achieve them.

Once you've decided on individual or group goals, and have written them in an acceptable format—specific, measurable, achievable, and challenging—you're ready to create an action plan to meet the objective.

Objectives are not achieved without planning and effort. To reach your final goal you must develop an action plan.

Time Management

Leaders are busy people. The more you take on responsibility, the more you invite people to give you responsibility. This means that if you wish to handle complex leadership roles, you must learn to manage your time.

What you do with your time is what you do with your life. It may be productive to sit quietly and ask yourself the following questions, considering each one carefully:

1. What are my three highest priorities for this week? This month? This year?

2. Are these consistent with my short and long-range goals?
3. How can I best organize my time for pay-offs in reaching these goals?
4. Where do I currently *owe* my time? Family? Profession? Friends?
5. What use of my time makes me happy? Is it related to my goals?
6. What are my major time wasters? Is there anything I can do to overcome them?
7. Am I willing to organize and discipline myself to make better use of my time?

Now that you have focused on your general use of time you might be interested in a few specific suggestions to save time. After reading these you may wish to add some of your own to the list.

How I Save Time

1. I don't waste time and energy feeling guilty about what I do.

2. If it's important, I will allow plenty of time to do it.

3. I try to find a new technique each day to help me gain time.

4. I review my short and long-range goals at least once each month.

5. I try to enjoy whatever I have decided to spend my time doing.

6. I carry 3 x 5 cards with me to jot down ideas when I am required to wait, stand in line, or when an appointment is canceled.

7. I make a list, in order of importance, of items I need to do each day. I revise it each morning.

8. I work smarter rather than harder.

9. I ask myself "What would happen if I did not do this?"

10. I cut off nonproductive activities as early as possible.

11. I make plenty of time to do high-priority tasks.

12. I concentrate on one thing at a time.

13. Anything that has long-term benefits I commit to paper for later revision and thought.

14. I set deadlines.

15. I try to listen well and learn it the first time.

16. I try not to waste other people's time.

17. I delegate everything I can to capable people.

18. I try to handle a piece of paper only once.

19. I write replies to some letters on the letters themselves.

20. I keep paperwork organized.

21. I try not to attend nonproductive meetings (or call them).

22. I allow periods of at least 15 minutes for relaxation during each three-hour period.

23. I persist when I believe I have a winner.

24. I try to do difficult or "dreaded" tasks early while I am fresh.

25. I try to never be rushed.

Assertiveness

Leaders must develop confidence, poise, decisiveness, and other characteristics associated with assertiveness. But it must be understood that assertive behavior is not the same as the aggressive behavior we associate with a rude or obnoxious person.

An assertive person has the ability to express the full range of his or her thoughts and emotions with confidence and skill. The aggressive person, on the other hand, overreacts, often creating defensive and angry listeners. The long-range effects of aggression are usually negative.

The following are suggestions for becoming positively assertive:

1. *Examine your voice and body actions for effective ways to express yourself with confidence.*
   - Use adequate volume in your voice. A voice that is too soft for the occasion may appear timid and uncertain. Speak up and speak clearly. Too much volume may suggest aggression, dominance, or anger.
   - Use a rate of speech appropriate to the occasion. A fast rate may cause you to appear nervous or rushed. On the other hand, a slow rate may appear uncertain and awkward. The average rate of speech is from 100 to 120 words per minute. Try reading a passage as you time it for rate. With practice you can maintain a reasonable rate of speech.
   - Be direct with your eye contact. Although you will not wish to stare a person down, look at them often enough to exhibit interest and confidence. If you avoid a certain amount of direct eye contact you may seem shy, bored, dishonest, or distracted. Most people expect you to look them in the eye often enough to demonstrate that you are involved mentally in the conversation.
   - Use appropriate facial expressions and body posture. It's hard to take a person seriously if they're smiling, laughing ner-

vously, or smirking. Often we're unaware of such habits as a clenched jaw, a frown, a distant gaze, or a critical snarl. Learn to make your facial expression reflective of your message. Examine your body posture. Assertive attitudes aren't usually expressed with slumped shoulders, nervous gestures, crouched sitting positions, or facing away from the other person. Again, coordinate your actions with your messages.

2. *Examine your methods for sharing feelings.*
   - If you find that you want to express a feeling with another person, be sure to find an appropriate time and place to do it. Effective assertiveness doesn't usually end in "blowing up" or in demonstrating severe anger or affection in public. On the other hand, it's a good idea to express emotions as early as you feel it's appropriate and will be received and heard.
   - Keep in mind that you're responsible for your own feelings. Others don't cause you to feel mad, sad, happy, and so on. Assertive communication is effective when you express your feelings in language that reflects these feelings belong to you. For instance, it's better to say "I'm angry over this" than to say "You make me angry," or "I am nervous in these interviews" rather than "You make me nervous."
   - Try to express your feelings briefly and to the point. We often use lengthy statements such as "I was more or less confused when you did not come to our meeting prepared to give the report you were scheduled to give." It might prove more to the point and certainly would be clearer to say "Why didn't you give your scheduled report?" or "I was embarrassed when you weren't prepared to give your report." In any case, be sure of the facts before you accuse or insist. If you're sure, then make your statement clearly, briefly, and frankly. Usually there's no need for apology or qualification, but you must remain sensitive to the person's feelings and the appropriateness of your statement.
   - It's confusing to others when we send coded messages. We often hide our true feelings in vague statements that confuse the listener and don't meet our needs. We might say "You're doing a pretty good job but all of us can use improvement" when you're trying to say "I like the work on the weekly report but I want to see a faster response to customer phone requests." Be specific.

3. *Feel free to change your mind or make mistakes.*
   - Remember that you're not irresponsible or unreliable merely because you changed your mind. It's often healthy and productive to change your mind if you find you're in error or you find a better way.

- If you make an error, admit it as soon as possible. Make any appropriate explanations to persons who may be involved and then forget it. It's normal to feel sorry for a mistake that hurt someone. Apologize, but don't feel subhuman for making the mistake.

4. *Try not to feel that everyone must like you.*
   - All of us like to be liked. It's unhealthy, however, to depend on everyone's love and admiration. In doing this we open ourselves to possible manipulation.
   - It's impossible to please everyone and any attempt at this is destined to fail. It makes life, and especially leadership, much easier and less stressful if we make honest attempts at mutual agreements with people but aren't addicted to always being successful.
   - In the same sense, we can't always "care" about everything and everyone around us. It's often impossible to *understand* much of what is happening much less *care* about it. Some things matter more to us than others and it's normal to reflect these preferences. We must remember not to condemn others and their views, but this appreciation and tolerance doesn't mean that we must express concern over all things and persons. To do so would be dishonest.

Developing assertiveness means that you think, speak, and act as if you, your ideas, and your feelings are as important as anyone else's. It's possible to assert yourself without infringing on the rights and feelings of others. It takes time and practice, but an effective leader would find the time well spent.

Listening

Effective listening is only accomplished through constant effort. Most people aren't willing to put out the effort required to become a truly effective listener. We might spend more energy on the skill, however, if we realize its importance.

According to research we understand only about one-half of what we hear. After a period of two months we recall only about one-quarter of what we heard. This is particularly discouraging when we realize that we spend 70 percent of every day in verbal communication and, of this, we spend 45 percent listening.

Although there are many reasons for ineffective listening there's one major reason for it: poor listening habits. We acquire most of these habits through daily casual conversation where habits of critical and comprehensive listening aren't required. If we're constantly critical or if we attempt to retain everything we hear, we're undertaking the impossible. On the other hand, if we understand that effective listening is acquired and not inherited, we may seek to acquire certain specific techniques that offer improvement. There are no quick and easy answers but the following techniques may get you started:

1. *Decide on your purpose for listening.* Are you listening for enjoyment, to discriminate between ideas or approaches, to learn information, to act as a sounding-board to a friend, or to critically evaluate and judge? All of these are good reasons to listen but will require different listening attitudes. Your purpose will usually be determined by your priorities at the time.

   It's hard to listen critically or to listen for learning when you're rushed or under stress. You may need to control your listening environment when listening effectiveness is critical. For instance, if you need to pass a course you should prepare for the listening experience by bringing note-taking materials and reading assignments, being on time, and arriving with a desire to learn. It's common for students to attend classes with the notion that they will learn by osmosis. They often aren't aware of the energy and attention required.

2. *Try not to assume you know what will be said before it is said.* We often develop bad habits of not listening because we assume it will be of no interest or use to us. We also make prior judgments about the amount of resistance or approval we will get from someone. With these prior notions we act without hearing or waiting to hear the speaker. We could improve our listening skills significantly by exercising patience and, even if we think we know what will be said, allow the speaker to finish.

3. *Try not to let your biases control your listening.* We all have certain prejudices and stereotypes that influence how we receive speakers. You may refuse to listen to someone because they are overdressed, foreign, overweight, too loud, too old, or even because they're opinionated. Attitudes such as this affect our listening habits by making us defensive and argumentative, or cause us to shut them out altogether.

4. *Try to monitor your listening through feedback.* Whenever possible, ask clear and thoughtful questions. If these questions are asked in the right spirit the speaker has an opportunity to repeat, expand, or clarify his or her message. Remember that you're the other half of the communication process and your reactions are critical to producing good communication for both you and the speaker.

5. *Learn to listen for the speaker's purpose.* This purpose may be stated or unstated. It's the basic reason the speaker has for speaking. We often assume early on that some speakers don't know why they're speaking. Often this is true but let's not be

too quick to judge. I have often found that a speaker who has some difficulty getting started, or who was a little disorganized, might recover and provide worthwhile information. Concentrate on what the speaker states as a purpose rather than what you have supposed is his or her purpose.

6. *Don't yield to distractions.* Our lives are noisy and confusing but we shouldn't use this as a convenient excuse for not listening. We can overcome some of the distraction by reducing noise and adjusting the listening environment. If we have no control over the distractions then we must rely on intense concentration to get as much as possible from the speaker.

7. *When possible, take notes.* If it's appropriate and it will not be distracting to the speaker, make a few notes as you listen. This will help you organize and frame the speaker's thoughts. It will also give you a reference to refer to at a later date if the material is technical or complex.

There is no communication skill more important to a leader than listening, yet many persons aspiring to be leaders neglect this skill. It seems to take so little effort to hear a speaker's words, but this isn't listening. The kind of practice we need in the techniques listed above will require that we monitor our habits and actively work to improve them.

Nonverbal Communication

Because meaning is conveyed both through words and through nonverbal means, such as vocal quality, expression, bodily action, and objects, the leader must also be a good nonverbal communicator.

Alfred Mehrabian says that we convey three types of information nonverbally:

- the sheer amount of reaction we have to the other person;
- our liking or disliking for them;
- power or submissiveness.
  Leaders should be able to monitor their communication nonverbally in all these areas.

First, it's important for leaders to show followers reaction. Too often leaders become inaccessible to those they lead because the leader's nonverbal communication to them indicates that he or she doesn't have interest in them. Often, simply by folding our arms, or glancing at a watch while we speak to another person, we may indicate that we don't have time or interest in their ideas. Eye contact also shows reaction, as well as facial reaction. When we are talking to others we should show attention and interest to them through all these means.

Second, leaders should be aware of the cues they send to others which show liking or disliking. It's inevitable that leaders will like some members of their groups better than others. However, it may be damaging to group morale if favorites become obvious to the group.

If we touch others, stand close to them, put ourselves on the same level, smile, and make eye contact, we are revealing warm feelings and closeness. If we pull away from others, stand apart, roll our eyes, or adopt a stern expression on our faces, it usually indicates disliking.

Leaders must be able to work with those people they don't like personally. Monitoring nonverbal reactions can make a working relationship more pleasant.

Finally, we can show our dominance or submission nonverbally. Sometimes leaders may want to emphasize their authority nonverbally to put down a challenge from someone. More often, however, leaders should be careful not to show too much dominance over those they lead, since domination may cause resentment from others.

Nonverbal actions that show dominance include standing over someone, looking down at them, invading another person's space, pointing fingers, giving less eye contact than is expected in return, object displays, and territoriality.

The leader who is careful about monitoring and controlling nonverbal messages will make sure the nonverbal communication doesn't conflict with the supportive climate that he or she is trying to create through verbal communication behaviors.

Working with Groups

The ability to work with groups is crucial for effective leadership. As we discussed in Chapter 3, groups have some unique advantages in solving problems and in performing some tasks. The interactions between group members produces unique solutions that no group member could have produced in isolation.

Groups sometimes run into roadblocks that keep them from being as effective as they could be in solving problems. The following are common problems in groups:

1. *Inadequate Procedure.* At times, groups don't use a systematic process in solving problems. As a result, they may try to adopt solutions before they have fully analyzed the problem. Or they may try to decide on solutions without any criteria against which to compare the proposed solutions. Groups may also decide on solutions without considering a broad enough range of alternatives. Finally, a group may rush to implement a solution without adequately considering its impact. All these problems could be avoided if group members followed a systematic process of problem solving, which will be described later in this chapter.

2. *Failure To Involve.* A group's advantages can only be realized when all the members make a full contribution. Sometimes shy members must be drawn out, or more aggressive members restrained so that everyone can talk and offer ideas.

3. *Inadequate Information.* Groups can hit roadblocks that halt progress if they aren't adequately prepared with pertinent information. For example, if you're planning for a dance, but no one checked to see what spaces are available, or what musical groups will cost, or how many people will come based on last year, you may have to call off the entire meeting. Decisions can't be made in the absence of important information.

4. *Rambling.* One of the most common problems groups face is keeping a topic focused on the problem at hand. Members have social needs, which stimulate conversation, sometimes on unrelated topics. One topic may suggest another topic, causing the discussion to wander. While a topic may be important to one member, it may divert the group as a whole from the discussion at hand. The group leader must keep the group focused on task, while still respecting the contributions of all members, making them feel important.

5. *Inadequate listening and feedback.* Sometimes members are so busy concentrating on the next thing they want to say, they fail to pay attention to the speaker. Even if they are listening, they may not give a verbal response. Imagine for a moment that you raise your hand to make a comment in class. After you finish, the teacher just goes ahead with the next topic in the lecture, as if you hadn't said a word. How would you feel? You might feel as if your comments weren't valued or important. Group members who aren't acknowledged, verbally and nonverbally, may have the same reaction.

6. *Improper balance of task and maintenance goals.* Groups exist to accomplish work and goals. They also exist to meet interpersonal needs for affiliation and socialization. This goal is called maintenance. Sometimes these two goals become unbalanced. We've all been part of groups that had a good time but never accomplished anything. We've also probably been in groups in which work became a drudgery. The group leader must work on the delicate balance of task and maintenance goals, keeping members directed toward task, but also making the work enjoyable and allowing members to meet social needs.

7. *Activity versus accomplishment.* Some groups manage to stay busy without managing to accomplish meaningful objectives. This may be because the work isn't well organized. Some work may be repetitive or unnecessary. Therefore, the criteria for evaluation of groups should not be how busy they are, but rather how much they actually accomplish.

8. *Failure to assign accountability.* Groups may be original and creative in their discussion of problems. Members may have wonderful ideas for solving problems, and yet if no one follows through with the ideas, they are meaningless. Therefore, it is important for the leader to make sure that good ideas are assigned to a specific individual who is responsible for carrying through with the idea. Not only should the leader make someone accountable for the project, but also the leader should follow through and check with the person after the meeting to make sure that the work is being accomplished.

Outline for Group Problem Solving

The obvious goal of group problem solving is to arrive at a solution to a problem. The solution is arrived at through a problem-solving sequence. The traditional sequence is as follows:

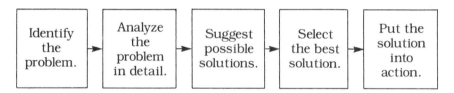

* **Identify the problem.** How do we know we have a problem? When fish die in our streams, birds die from breathing our air, and plants die from lack of sunlight, we have symptoms of a pollution problem. When the high school band plays fewer and fewer pep songs during a game, the student fans aren't cheering the team, and there's a drop in attendance at the games, we have symptoms of a "lack of school spirit" problem.

The group must decide if the symptoms are serious enough to warrant a study of the problem. If it is decided that the problem is serious and deserves the group's attention, then still another question must be asked: "Is this a problem for our group?" Often the problem is outside the power and resources of the group and either must be dropped or passed on to another group that can solve it. In some cases the problem is one that will correct itself if given time.

* **Analyze the problem.** What caused the problem? We can often be more successful if we treat the cause rather than the symptoms. We can't end campus demonstrations merely by stopping the demonstrators with armed guards or requiring parade permits. We must consider the root causes and attempt to eliminate them. We can't correct pollution by cleaning up the beaches, restocking the rivers with fish, and planting more trees. We will temporarily erase the out-

ward symptoms, but the pollution will still be there and will appear again in the same form until we eliminate the cause.

Some groups are wise enough to realize that they can't solve all problems. After a careful study of a problem they may decide that the problem isn't worth their time, can be better solved by another group or individual, or should be considered at a more appropriate time. Although we hesitate to delay action on a problem, we may find that the group will make a better and more satisfying decision if it's delayed.

• **Suggest possible solutions.** The best method is to "brainstorm" for all possible courses of action. This is done by suggesting all solutions that come to mind regardless of how impractical or absurd they may sound. After they're all listed, the group can compare them and select a shorter list. Study the possibilities for compromises (combining two or more solutions, eliminating one solution in favor of another one, and so on.). Next, make up a final list of solutions.

• **Select a solution.** Consider such questions as: Is it the best solution for all persons concerned? How difficult will it be to accomplish? Will it correct the cause and not merely the symptoms? Will it require much time and money?

For example: a student council seeks a way to raise funds for bringing famous lecturers to the school. Many methods are suggested, including a student car wash, magazine sales, cake sale, a giant garage sale, or a new student activities fee. Any of these might raise the necessary funds but the group must deliberate carefully and choose one that, when adopted, will be the most acceptable to the various interests—the student body, the student council, the faculty, the administration, and the parents. It's often impossible to please everyone, but the best choice would be one that pleases as many as possible and at the same time raises the necessary funds.

• **Take action.** This may be an easy task if it's implied by the solution. If a student council decides to form two new standing committees for the coming year, the procedure might be as simple as having the president appoint the committees and announce the names to the council. If the council decided to institute an honor system for the student body, the implementation step would be a difficult one. The council should meet and convince the faculty, administration, student body, and perhaps even the parents of its value. This would require careful planning.

With the problem-solving sequence firmly in mind, the leader can turn to questions of how he or she can get the group to work together successfully. The following are suggestions for improving communication in the small group.

• **Develop a strong relationship among group members.** People don't like to be treated as "numbers" or "positions." The leader can make a point of finding out about the goals, fears, hopes, and conditions of his members. People are flattered when you know personal things about them, but this must not be artificial. If the leader doesn't really care, it will usually become evident. Get to know your members. Anticipate their reactions and understand their views.

- **Make the group's work important.** People don't like to be a part of a stale, backward organization. They like teamwork. If the leader has doubts about the importance of the group task, he will have difficulty in getting the enthusiasm and cooperation he wants. Avoid asking a person to chair a committee by telling her "Oh, you won't have to do much, the committee doesn't meet often and practically runs itself."

It's also a good idea to develop a "tradition" in the group. This isn't always easy to do and must never be forced. As the leader sees opportunities he or she should emphasize the group's contributions and progress. Such events as parties, initiation ceremonies, and installation services help in developing "tradition" and add a feeling of permanence.

An occasional restatement of the group goals will also remind the group of the importance of its work. This can be done in many ways but one easy method is to relate all new projects and decisions to the stated group goals. For instance, if a student council has decided to organize a student faculty dance in order to raise money for its projects, the president may, at a business meeting, mention in a complimentary manner the excellent work of the committee and how its efforts contribute to the council's stated goal of developing better student-faculty relations.

- **Reward members for good work.** These rewards can, of course, take the form of prizes and gifts, but more important are the small compliments and other gestures of appreciation and recognition. Let individual members know that without their efforts the group would not be as successful. Avoid praising only the persons with higher status positions. Their contributions may seem to be more important at the moment, but true cohesiveness is better achieved by making all members feel rewarded for good work.

- **Plan meetings carefully.** The good leader will do his or her homework and will be ready for the meeting. Prepare needed materials ahead of time and distribute them to the members. Secure an acceptable meeting place with a proper environment for your meeting. The effectiveness of a five-member committee can be reduced by meeting in the first row of seats in a 500-seat theater. This may sound obvious, but many leaders are unaware of the dramatic effect environment has on meetings. Poor lighting, interruptions, ringing telephones, crowded rooms, or poor heating or air-conditioning could become distractions that hurt the effectiveness of the meeting.

The type of meeting you want must also be planned. Members must know not only what they are expected to accomplish but the method to be used in conducting the meeting. Will the meeting be held to brief the members? Will it be a planning meeting? These are usually informal and require a great deal of time. A student council may wish to have one or two of these meetings at the beginning of the school year.

Still another type of meeting is the problem-solving meeting. If the group knows it's meeting to solve a problem, the mental attitudes of the members should be geared toward decision making.

We often misjudge a meeting because we didn't understand its purpose. The purpose can be announced or it can become a "tradition" or "ritual" of the organization.

Once it becomes a tradition, the members will recognize its purpose and act accordingly. For instance, the first business meeting of the year for a student council may be a ritual in that much of the time may be spent in re-introducing the officers, reminding members of committee tasks, and welcoming everyone to a new year.

Here are a few suggestions for conducting a small group meeting:

- Get the meeting started on time.

- Keep the discussion on the topic.

- Try for balanced participation, encouraging contributions by all members.

- Try to keep one or two members from monopolizing the meeting.

- Use questions and summaries to keep the meeting moving in a positive and constructive direction.

- At the close of the meeting, summarize what has been said and announce any decisions reached.

Motivating

Our approach to motivation may be different from many that you have read in the past. Many writers consider motivation as a *leader* skill, something that the leader does to followers. We would like to discuss motivation as a characteristic of followers.

Followers have internal motivations that they bring to tasks. Leaders must understand and work with the motivations that followers already have.

Motivation, then, is a matter of meeting the needs of followers. In Chapter 3 we discussed Schutz's system of interpersonal needs. He said that people have needs for affection, for control, and for inclusion. In Chapter 4 we discussed McClelland's system of motivations. He argues that individuals are motivated by achievement, by power, and by affiliation. Drawing on these concepts of interpersonal needs, the leader should understand that:

1. Individuals come to tasks and to groups with needs they hope to have fulfilled.
2. Individuals differ in the needs that are most dominant for them.

Leaders, to enhance motivation, must understand the predominant needs of the followers. For example, the leader must understand if the group is primarily motivated by achievement of tasks or by social contacts with others.

Next, the leader must present the tasks to be accomplished in a way that meets the needs of the followers. For example, if you want to recruit a large number of your group to serve as volunteers in a fundraising event, you might present the job in two different ways depending on whether group members are motivated by achievement or affiliation.

If your group has high needs for affiliation you might stress how much fun the group will have working together in planning for the fundraiser, and how many different people they will meet during the event. If your group is motivated primarily by achievement, you should stress how much money can be raised, and how much can be accomplished for the worthwhile charity.

Either strategy may gain cooperation, depending on the characteristics of your group.

In addition to meeting the needs of followers, the leader should consider two other communication behaviors to create a productive climate. The first type of communication that is helpful is what we refer to as "positive management." This simply means that the leader should give positive comments to followers.

Too often we tend to focus on the mistakes and things that aren't done correctly. Sometimes we forget to comment on jobs that are done well, or on people who are giving their best effort. Researchers have found that positive feedback is much more productive than negative in producing changes in behavior. If you can find a way to compliment followers rather than criticizing their work, they will have a much greater incentive to work for you in the future.

A second behavior that tends to increase motivation is supportive communication. Jack Gibbs has written that some types of communication create defensive reactions, while others create a supportive climate.[1]

If you act *superior* to others, they may resent you and feel inferior. But if you act *equal*, members may respect you more.

If you are *dogmatic* and act like you know everything, then people will look for ways to prove you wrong. If you are more *provisional* about your judgments, however, it will be easier for others to listen to you.

1. Jack Gibb, "Defensive Communication," *Journal of Communication,* 11 (1961), 141-148.

If you try to *control* others and force them to do what you want, they will respond less favorably than if you involve them in *problem solving*.

If you use *evaluative* or judgmental language in talking to others, they may feel you are attacking them. But if you use more *descriptive* language, they can respond less emotionally.

If you remain detached and *neutral* with others, instead of showing *empathy*, then the follower may not identify with you as strongly.

Finally, if you seem to *manipulate* others instead of being *honest* with them, their trust in you may be diminished.

Here are a few more motivational tips for leaders who want their groups to be more productive:

1. Help followers see the big picture and understand how each effort contributes to the total goal.
2. Individualize your efforts toward motivation. Try to find out what is motivating to each individual and try to present the task in a way that meets those needs.
3. Give positive feedback.
4. Give members a sense of control and initiative over their work. Ask their opinions on matters that concern them.
5. Create a positive climate.
6. Encourage risk taking. Only when members feel that mistakes will not be punished will they take risks to be innovative, creative, and responsible.

Managing Conflict

Since conflict is such an inevitable part of any human activity, leaders must be equipped to manage conflicts constructively. Often we think of conflict as something unpleasant and undesirable. Our first instinct is to avoid it. But such a tendency is unrealistic, and may be harmful.

Conflict can sometimes perform needed functions for a group. It can bring a problem out into the open so that solutions can be found. It can force needed change. Finally, conflict can actually help relationships by getting disagreements into the open instead of letting them fester inside.

● *Defining Conflict.*

Conflict occurs whenever two or more parties sense conflicting goals. Let's analyze this definition. First, two parties must have some interdependence in order to have conflict. If I don't depend on you for anything, it's unlikely we would ever be in conflict. Second, conflicts usually occur over incompatible goals or scarce resources. Scarce resources are finite things like money or time or awards. Incompatible

56

goals occur whenever you block at least part of something someone else wants.

Finally, it's also important to note that one only has to *perceive* incompatible goals or scarce resources for conflict to exist. Sometimes our perceptions aren't accurate, yet we will experience conflict if we believe them to be true.

• *Types of Conflict.*

One type of conflict is competitive (also called win-lose or zero-sum). One person must win and one person must lose. It usually exists in a situation with scarce resources. There's just so much to go around, and if I get what I want, you can't get all you want.

A second type of conflict is lose-lose. Sometimes we fight so hard to win in a situation that the conflict becomes destructive, and everyone involved loses. Often divorces or child custody cases may be fought in such a climate of bitterness that both parties destroy each other.

A last and more positive type of conflict is win-win or cooperative. In this situation, goals may seem incompatible at the outset, but as people work together in a spirit of cooperation, they find ways to reach both of their goals simultaneously.

Perhaps because we are so competitive in our society, we sometimes view situations as win-lose or competitive when they could be conducted in other ways. For example, we view another competent member in our group as a threat because we want others to respect and look up to us. We feel that if the group begins to respect someone else, then it will diminish our own leadership. However, there is no reason why this situation really has to be competitive.

Respect is not a scarce resource. The fact that group members look up to one person doesn't mean that they think any less of the other. Yet we may perceive it that way.

It's important that leaders be able to assess conflict situations to determine if they really are competitive, or whether they might be handled in a more cooperative way.

Just as there are different types of conflict, there are a variety of styles for dealing with conflict. The following are several approaches that could be taken:

1. *Accommodation*—This means that one side gives in without requesting or expecting any concessions from the other.

2. *Avoidance*—Here the individual avoids any situation that may have the potential for conflict, even if it means that he has to hold anger inside.

3. *Compromise*—Both parties give in on part of what they want in order to reach an agreement that will end the conflict.

4. *Competition*—This person fights hard to win. Not only does the person want to win, but he also wants the other party to lose.
5. *Collaboration*—In this style, both parties in a conflict engage in problem solving to find ways to reach a solution that gives both parties all they want.

Probably all of us can think of situations in which we use different styles to solve conflicts. Yet, we may be able to identify one that we use more than others. You may want to assess if your conflict style is beneficial for you by asking the following questions:

1. *Do I get what I want by acting in this way?* Avoiding or being accommodating in conflicts may feel comfortable, but you may begin to realize that you are losing positions or rewards that you really want. Over time this may make you feel resentful or angry.
2. *Do I harm others by acting this way?* At times we may be getting our own way a great deal by acting competitively. At the same time we may be achieving our goals at the expense of another's pride or self-respect. We may also be achieving our victories at the expense of relationships that are important to us.
3. *Am I enacting my conflict style out of choice, or because I don't know any other way to behave?* Conflict management is enhanced when you have a variety of options and can choose the most appropriate way to behave. If you're in a competitive situation, it may be most appropriate to mirror a competitive style. At times it may be important to know how to give in graciously— when you are wrong or when the issue is not important to you.

Any of the styles may be most appropriate in a given situation, so it's important to be flexible.

Hocker and Wilmot in their book, *Interpersonal Conflict*, suggest several types of communication especially helpful in managing conflict constructively.[2] They include:

1. *Description*—Making non-evaluative statements about observable events without attributing motives or making judgments.
2. *Qualification*—Stating clearly what are and are not the issues to be resolved.
3. *Disclosure*—Getting thoughts, feelings, intentions, motivations, and past history out into the open in an honest and nondefensive manner.
4. *Soliciting Disclosure*—Asking for information from the other party about events related to the conflict that can't be observed.
5. *Negative Inquiry*—Soliciting complaints about oneself, and being open to constructive criticism.

2. Joyce L. Hocker and William W. Wilmot, *Interpersonal Conflict*, 2nd ed., Dubuque, Ia.: William C. Brown, Publishers, 1985, pp. 115-122.

6. *Empathy or Support*—Expressing understanding, acceptance, or positive regard for another person even when you don't agree with his position.
7. *Emphasizing Commonalities*—Commenting on shared interests, goals, or compatibilities with another person despite acknowledgment of the conflict.
8. *Accepting Responsibility*—Attributing responsibility for conflicts to self or both parties.
9. *Initiating Problem Solving*—Initiating mutually acceptable solutions to conflict, with serious consideration of any alternative suggested by either party.

All of these communication behaviors imply an openness and willingness to reach out to the other person. In order for conflicts to be managed productively, both parties must have this collaborative approach to conflict.

Here are a few more tips about dealing with conflict:

1. Everyone has blind spots. Recognize the role of perception and assumption in conflict situations.
2. Focus on understanding the problem before developing solutions.
3. Focus on superordinate goals that both parties have in common rather than the smaller differences.
4. Realize that you can win a battle and lose the war.
5. Use supportive communication behaviors appropriate for a cooperative approach to conflict.
6. Be specific. Identify the particular belief, behavior, attitude, or value at issue.
7. Don't assume you know what the other person is thinking or feeling.
8. Take your time. Don't respond without thinking. Clarify your thoughts.
9. Don't attempt to handle too many issues at once.
10. Pick a time and mutually acceptable place.
11. Don't attack the other person's self-esteem and identity.
12. Don't be afraid to admit that you are wrong, and permit the other person to admit gracefully that he was wrong.
13. Don't assume the conflict is over until both parties say so.

Speaking in Public

The concept of public speaking has undergone significant changes in the past 10 to 15 years. The silver-tongued orator or the use of a flamboyant style denotes speakers of the past.

Today's audiences seek speakers who address themselves to everyday problems in a direct, communicative, and conversational manner.

The speaker's platform is no longer a place to perform or exhibit clear diction; it is, instead, a social opportunity to influence behavior and attitudes.

Leaders are called upon to speak in public for various reasons: to perform public relations for an organization, to solicit support for a group's cause, or to present current thinking on a subject or problem. In any case, leaders are expected to "play the role of speaker."

The speaker's role has the following basic parts: the helper, the informer, and the persuader. Although all three are essential to playing the full role of speaker, the "helper" is the most significant.

● *The Speaker as Helper.*

The world is full of speakers competing for the attention of listeners. But successful speakers are those who develop a helping relationship between themselves and their audiences.

Rather than centering attention on a topic of special interest to the speaker, it's better to concentrate on something worthwhile for the audience.

The leader should ask, "How can I best be of service to this group on this occasion, and furthermore, how can I communicate to them my intention of serving their needs?" Answering this question satisfactorily is the best attention-getting device available.

Speakers must first make an analysis of their audience. They must determine audience needs as *they* see them. This is not an easy task but is worth the time and effort.

We are all aware of what happens when no attempt is made to analyze the audience. Teachers who do not understand their students often aim too low or too high. They are either too "academic" or they insult the intelligence of many of the students.

In the same manner, students speaking to the local P.T.A. may fail to achieve their purpose due to lack of audience analysis. If they intend to seek support for a student council fundraising activity and don't realize that a large majority of the businesspeople present opposed the same project two years ago, they probably won't meet with success. If they had known, they might have changed their appeal to another activity or made a new and more acceptable approach to the controversial activity.

The "audience-oriented" approach is a far better technique for holding interest than is a series of jokes, stories, or statistics. Use a direct and friendly attitude to communicate that you feel confident your speech will be worth listening to.

● *The Speaker as Informer.*

One of the obvious reasons for listening to any speaker is to gain information. If the audience feels that the speaker is a good source of information they will give the deserved attention. If speakers know the subject thoroughly and demonstrate a desire to share the information, they will command the respect of the audience.

A leader holds a position of authority. While in this position he or she gains information and insights that should be shared. The leader may be asked by the group to offer ideas and observations on a current topic or to share experiences with an outside group. In each case the leader becomes a resource person and is expected to share information clearly and accurately.

It may be a good idea to take a "meat and potatoes" approach to being an informational speaker. This means that you must have something worthwhile to say. The substance of the speech may very well be the most important consideration. This may take the form of new ideas, new information, a new slant on an old idea, or a new interpretation of existing information.

In a well-planned speech, the speaker develops a single theme. He or she develops this theme with specific examples, definitions, comparisons, statistics, and anecdotes. These are the "meat and potatoes" of the speech.

When selecting the information you will release, use items based on relevance, accuracy, and human interest. If your information is current and directed to this specific audience, it will gain appeal. If it is accurate, you will have more confidence in the data and will reflect this in your speech. Finally, if you understand how appealing a story can be to an audience you can gain human interest. People love action, emotion, conflict, novelty, and old items with a new twist. These will provide the excitement of human interest.

- *The Speaker as Persuader.*

When leaders wish to change the attitudes, beliefs, values, or behavior of an audience, they become persuaders. There's no reason to draw a sharp distinction between informing and persuading since both will be used by effective speakers. The following are a few suggestions for the leader-persuader.

1. *Use evidence to support your arguments.* Don't expect people to accept something merely because you said it. Personal opinion is useful as long as it's designated as such and not stated as fact. If you state that a majority of students at your school support the student council, you must either support this statement with evidence (polls taken, random samples, or surveys), or qualify the statement as your opinion ("it is my opinion that a majority . . .").

   Evidence is useful in establishing the credibility of your statements. Evidence usually takes these forms: direct quotes, statistics, examples, reports of research, and reports of surveys and polls.

2. *Remember that people do things for their reasons and not for yours.* When you search for arguments and evidence, be sure to seek ideas and materials that will serve as "proof" to your audience and not solely to yourself. You may have the best of reasons for your beliefs and actions but they may not be the same as those of your audience.

3. *Determine your specific purpose before you prepare the speech.* Do you intend to merely stir up the already favorable feelings the audience has about a subject, or do you intend to go a step further and convince them to change their beliefs? Study your listeners and determine a realistic purpose that can be achieved within the limits of time, audience interest, audience prior knowledge, and the occasion. For example, it would be next to impossible to persuade a group of smokers to give up smoking with a 20-minute speech. A more realistic goal would be to persuade them that there is substantial evidence to indicate a relationship between lung cancer and smoking.

4. *Avoid negative suggestions.* Try to make all remarks in a positive manner. The salesman who says "You don't need any insurance, do you?" probably won't make many sales. Remarks such as "I don't think many of you are going to agree with me," and "I don't know much about this myself" will defeat a speaker's purpose in persuasion. They might be replaced with "I realize the controversial nature of this subject" or "I became interested in this subject only last month, but since that time I have read a few articles I would like to share with you today."

5. *It's best to present both sides of a controversial issue when talking to persons opposed to your point of view.* The opposition is often "put at ease" when you seem well aware of their side and take it into consideration when you present your point of view. If you present only your side, the opposition may mistakenly believe that you are ill-informed or unaware that there is another side to the argument.

6. *As much persuasion is achieved by a speaker's personal character as by his verbal message.* We believe the people we consider "good" and often won't listen to the ones we consider "bad." The judgment as to who is good varies from person to person. If a speaker appears trustworthy and able, he's won half the battle. Some of his character and expertise is determined prior to his speech by his reputation with the audience. If a person has not yet achieved a good reputation, he can establish one by being well-prepared and practiced, adapting his speech to his audience, demonstrating confidence and ease, and showing respect for the audience and their ideas.

- *How To Prepare and Organize Your Speech.*

After you have made an analysis of your audience you're ready to begin preparing your speech. Although there's no magic formula, there are some basic steps that most speakers use:

1. *Determine your purpose.* Decide whether you will inform or persuade, and what kind of specific reaction you want from your audience.
2. *Select a topic to achieve your purpose.* For instance, if you decide to persuade your audience to vote in the next campus election, you must choose a topic suited to achieving that purpose. You could speak on "voter responsibility," "the need for a better student government," "the candidates and their platforms," or "urgent needs at our school."
3. *Select an appropriate organizational pattern.* The traditional pattern includes an introduction, the body (including main points), and a conclusion.
4. *Prepare the body of the speech in a detailed outline.*
5. *Prepare the introduction and conclusion in a detailed outline.*
6. *Practice the speech from the detailed outline and make final changes* that are needed to make it sound appropriate and clear to the audience. This is an important step since a written outline may use a stilted style of language inappropriate to oral discourse.
7. *Prepare speaking notes from your detailed outline.* With the full outline in mind you can now prepare the brief set of notes you will need as you deliver the speech.
8. *Practice using speaking notes.*

- *The Use of Voice and Gesture.*

Today's speakers are expected to be informal and conversational in delivery. They should develop an attitude of directness, including effective eye contact, concrete language, forceful but appropriate gestures, and an "intimate" vocal tone. They should appear composed and confident without appearing too "cool" or detached. They should talk to the audience in the same earnest manner they use in lively conversation. The attention of the audience should be drawn away from the speaker's voice and directed to the ideas. This informal manner seems to communicate goodwill and friendliness.

Exaggerated gestures, awkward mannerisms, and poor posture should be avoided.

Learning the principles of public speaking will not ensure your success as a speaker. These ideas provide a good beginning, but you will need experience in various public speaking situations to refine and develop your skills. Most good speakers look for every opportunity to further improve their skills.

Using Parliamentary Procedure

Nearly everyone, but especially leaders, will find a need for the basic principles of organizing and conducting meetings. We're fortunate that people with experience in various types of organizations have provided us with a universal set of rules for meetings.

Thomas Jefferson prepared the first parliamentary manual and, in so doing, demonstrated that our organizations can be "democracy in miniature." Jefferson's rules were modified and expanded by Henry M. Robert in 1876. *Robert's Rules of Order* then became one of the first manuals for parliamentary procedure. The latest revision of Robert's manual was *Robert's Rules of Order, Newly Revised,* 1970. This book is probably the single most popular book on the subject in America.

There will be times in your meetings when you will ask yourself if parliamentary procedure isn't just a set of rules designed to stymie meetings, more of a barrier to discussion than an aid. This is a popular notion and may be somewhat justified.

With groups of 12 or fewer it might be more practical and efficient to use group discussion methods, but even these groups will unconsciously use such basic procedures as voting, making motions, and addressing the chair. Their usual comment is that they aren't using parliamentary procedure, but anyone examining their deliberations will soon notice that they have simply adapted the basic procedure to suit the needs of their group. This is the way it should be.

The larger the group the more often we find a formal set of rules being followed. Large groups tend to get unruly due to diverse opinions. These groups need a procedure that allows the majority to rule. At the same time, they need something that protects the rights of the minority.

The best and most efficient method yet devised for achieving this is the use of parliamentary procedure. It guards against hasty action, gives each person a chance to be heard, provides for order, and ensures majority rule.

A few general points deserve emphasis before we discuss the core procedure. For example, we mentioned earlier that small groups might use the group discussion method. We recommend this procedure for committee deliberations or for organizations that have so few members consensus is possible and desirable.

If committees take their job seriously, there is less need for debate on critical motions in the general meetings. It's the duty of the committee to research the matters referred to it and to make recommendations to the organization. This is not to say that all actions proposed by committees should be accepted. The committee should make its report and await the group's reaction. If the group agrees with the report, then all is well; but if they disagree and decide to amend the report, this is their right and the committee should cooperate fully.

Another point of emphasis concerns the proposals made by members of committees. These motions should be made as accurately as possible. It's a good idea to have all motions written, read, and then immediately passed to the secretary or chairman for the sake of accuracy and time economy. A majority of your motions should come from committee deliberations.

Most controversies and misunderstandings are due to a lack of information. It's important, therefore, to keep members informed by providing them with pertinent facts that they can study before the deliberations start. Often, a conscientious person will refuse to vote without proper information.

It's helpful to prepare a detailed agenda for each meeting and to give it to all members before the meeting. The agenda should include a listing of all items of business to come before the group, along with explanations of those items that might be controversial or misunderstood. In addition, the agenda should include a list of all committees whose reports are due (and the names of the committee chairpersons), and reminders of actions taken at the last meeting.

Such an agenda would not only create interest but might also promote attendance and act as a good promotional document for the organization. Anyone seeing it would realize that the group was active and working. Committee chairpersons, after seeing their name on the agenda, might have a renewed interest in carrying out their duties.

Finally, it's imperative that the members of the organization be trained in the use of parliamentary procedure. This training must include not only practice in the procedure's actual techniques, but also (to encourage a respect for the rules) a study of the philosophy behind the procedure. Here are a few recommendations concerning this training.

- The president should study the procedure privately and inspire a respect for the procedure by conducting the meetings properly and efficiently.
- The organization should appoint a good parliamentarian. This could be either a student, or an adult who is capable and prepared to act as a resource person and a critic of the procedure.
- Employ, at first, only the procedure that the members can use; move to the more complicated procedure as the members grow in their knowledge of its proper use.
- Train the membership through such methods as workshops, mock meetings, demonstrations, and drills.
- Have all the leaders in your organization attend conferences and workshops provided at the state and national level.
- Work to create in all meetings an atmosphere in which members feel free to use the procedure.
- Never be satisfied with a procedure that doesn't provide for an orderly and efficient meeting. Remember that it may take months

or years before a satisfactory procedure is accepted by the organization.

• Provide your members with a variety of reference materials on parliamentary procedure. The reading list in the back of this book suggests some of these materials.

• *The Core Procedure.*

Don't make it more complicated than it is. There are only five aspects of parliamentary procedure that must be understood to get along well in meetings. In unusual circumstances you may have to look up information in *Robert's Rules*, but not often. Study the following five aspects of the procedure carefully. This is about all you will need to conduct or participate in most meetings.

1. *Presiding Over a Meeting.* To conduct meetings properly you must keep order, stay with an agenda, ensure proper procedure, and see that the rights of all members are protected. Parliamentary procedure will not provide order for you. You must have the respect of the group. Your only responsibility is to be well-informed and fair in your dealings with the members.

A group may refuse to conduct itself in an orderly manner. Restoring order is as much their responsibility as yours. Use your powers of diplomacy and fair play. If this fails, call the meeting "adjourned" until order can be restored. It's unlikely that you will find many groups that will not respond to an honest appeal for order. Don't be impatient and angry if they are disorderly at times—such is the nature of people. Conduct yourself as a servant of the group's decisions and you will have much success conducting meetings.

The general order of business for meetings is as follows: call to order, reading and approval of minutes, reports of standing committees, reports of special committees, unfinished business, new business, announcements, and adjournment.

This list of eight steps should be adjusted to meet the needs of your meetings. You may wish to set up your own agenda steps (with approval of the group). The chairperson's responsibility is to encourage an efficient and smooth movement through the agenda.

You must be well informed on the core procedure so that you can answer members' questions. This does not mean that you must memorize *Robert's Rules*. Even the best presiding officers have occasions when they must refer to *Robert's Rules* or to someone knowledgeable on the subject of the procedure. No one expects you to have all the answers, but most groups expect you to have a working knowledge of the procedure.

Your most important function while presiding is to ensure

fairness and to protect members' rights. If you use parliamentary procedure correctly you will find that a good deal of this is built into the procedure for you. On those occasions when there is no appropriate rule you must apply the rules of "fairness." Make your rulings on the basis of what is just and fair for all persons involved.

2. *Making Main Motions.* You make a motion by addressing the chair (Mr./Madam Chair), receiving recognition ("Mr. Jones"), and saying "I move that . . ." The presiding officer must then secure a second and open the floor for discussion.

During this discussion period the motion can be debated, amended, referred to a committee, or delayed; even a motion to "adjourn" is in order. If you don't adjourn, delay, or refer, and there is no further discussion, then the discussion is declared "closed" by the presiding officer and a call for the vote is taken.

A simple majority vote is required for the motion to pass. This means that one more than one-half of the members present *and voting* must vote *for* the motion in order for it to pass. For instance, if there are 30 members present and the vote count is five affirmative and two negative, the motion passes. It doesn't require that the other 23 members vote. Note that this is true with any motion requiring a simple majority vote unless a group's constitution states otherwise.

After the vote is completed the chair announces the vote and then turns to the next item of business. For rules used in amending a motion, consult pp. 108-140 in *Robert's Rules of Order, Newly Revised.*

3. *Making Special Motions.* There are approximately 26 special motions used in most meetings. They are relatively easy to understand and learn. The following list provides the motion, its purpose, and page numbers from *Robert's Rules of Order, Newly Revised* for further reference. Study each one carefully and then use this list as a reference in meetings.

A List of Basic Motions

1. *Adjourn*—To close the meeting (199-207).
2. *Amend*—To propose a change or modification in a main motion (108-140).
3. *Appeal from the decision of the chair*—To appeal to the assembly to override a ruling made by the chair (213-214, 218-222).
4. *Committee of the whole*—To consider a motion informally, using group discussion methods (442-450).
5. *Division of the assembly*—To ask for a re-vote by means which would produce a readily distinguishable division between "yes" and "no" votes (237-239).

6. *Fix the time to which to adjourn*—To set a time for reassembling (207-211).
7. *Lay on the table*—To postpone consideration of a question temporarily (177-185, 253-254, 322-323).
8. *Limit debate*—To restrict the time or number of speakers for debate on a motion (161-166).
9. *Main motion*—To propose action concerning the general business of an organization (46-47, 82-104).
10. *Special order of business*—To set a specific time for the exclusive consideration of a particular question (309-311).
11. *Object to consideration*—To object to the consideration of a motion considered irrelevant or objectionable (227-229, 423-424).
12. *Orders of the day*—To request that the group conform to the order of business (186-191).
13. *Parliamentary inquiry*—To seek advice from the chair concerning parliamentary procedure (245).
14. *Point of information*—To request information concerning pending business (245-246).
15. *Point of order*—To call attention to an error in parliamentary procedure (212-218).
16. *Postpone indefinitely*—To dispose of a motion without voting on it (105-108).
17. *Postpone to a certain time*—To delay until a specified time any action upon a pending question (150-161).
18. *Previous question*—To terminate discussion on a debatable motion by bringing it to an immediate vote (166-177).
19. *Question of privilege*—A request for the chair to deal with an emergency situation (191-196).
20. *Recess*—To temporarily disband for a specific purpose (196-199).
21. *Reconsider*—To give the group an opportunity to consider again a vote already taken (265-281).
22. *Refer or commit*—To delay action or investigate further a question by referring it to a committee (140-150).
23. *Rescind*—To cancel an action taken at a previous meeting (256-260).
24. *Suspend the rules*—To make possible for a temporary period a procedure contrary to the standing rules (222-227).
25. *Take from the table, or Resume consideration*—To revive a motion previously laid on the table, or temporarily put aside (180-181).
26. *Withdraw a motion*—To prevent action on a motion when the maker of the motion has changed his mind (246-248).

The following is a reference chart for the basic motions. It is designed for quick reference during meetings.

Quick-Reference Parliamentary Procedure Chart

IN ORDER OF PRECEDENCE

	Second Needed	Amendable	Debatable	Vote Required	Interrupt Speaker
Fix time of next meeting	Yes	Yes	No	½	No
Adjourn	Yes	No	No	½	No
Recess	Yes	Yes	No	½	No
Question of privilege	No	No	No	ch.	Yes
Lay on the table	Yes	No	No	½	No
Previous question	Yes	No	No	⅔	No
Limit debate	Yes	Yes	No	⅔	No
Postpone to a certain time	Yes	Yes	Yes	½	No
Refer to a committee	Yes	Yes	Yes	½	No
Committee of the whole	Yes	Yes	Yes	½	No
Amend	Yes	Yes	*	½	No
Postpone indefinitely	Yes	No	Yes	½	No

NO ORDER OF PRECEDENCE

	Second Needed	Amendable	Debatable	Vote Required	Interrupt Speaker
Main motion	Yes	Yes	Yes	½	No
Take from table	Yes	No	No	½	No
Reconsider	Yes	No	*	½	Yes
Rescind	Yes	Yes	Yes	⅔	No
Make special order of business	Yes	Yes	Yes	⅔	No
Appeal from decision of chair	Yes	No	*	⅔	No
Suspend the rules	Yes	No	No	½	Yes
Object to consideration	No	No	No	⅔	No
Parliamentary inquiry	No	No	No	ch.	Yes
Withdraw a motion	No	No	No	ch.	Yes
Division	No	No	No	½	No
Point of order	No	No	No	½	Yes
Request for information	No	No	No	½	No

* Debatable when motion to which it applies is debatable.
ch. The chairman can make the decision, but is a majority vote if appealed.

4. *Keeping records of meetings.* It is essential that you keep an accurate record of your meetings. This is done through the "minutes." The secretary keeps this record and members approve of the previous meeting's minutes. The following is a suggested outline for minutes:

   1. Name of the organization.
   2. Date, hour, place, and kind of meeting.
   3. Names of regular chairman and secretary if they were present or names of their substitutes.
   4. Whether the minutes of the previous meeting were read and approved—as read or as corrected.
   5. Each main motion and the name of the person making it. State whether the motion passed or failed and give the vote on the question.
   6. All points of order and appeals whether sustained or lost along with the chairman's response to the ruling.
   7. Special motions which might be of concern and/or interest in future meetings (at discretion of secretary).
   8. Time and method of adjournment.
   9. Signature of the secretary.

   Do not summarize the discussion that took place at the meeting or make value judgments about events transpiring during the meeting. You may include a brief summary of committee reports instead of placing the entire report in the minutes. (See *Robert's Rules of Order, Newly Revised,* pages 389-392.)

5. *Electing officers and using your constitution and by-laws.* The rules regarding these activities vary from one organization to another. Refer to *Robert's Rules of Order, Newly Revised* for more information. See pp. 368-389 for election of officers and pp. 474-498 for constitution and by-laws.

Appendix

SUGGESTIONS AND EXERCISES FOR DEVELOPING LEADERSHIP SKILLS

Self-Improvement

1. Check the reading list at the end of this book for books in the areas of communication theory. Read as many of these as possible and share them with members of your student council.
2. Choose a leader in your community who you admire. Spend a week observing and studying his or her behavior. Try to attend events where he or she will appear, read anything he or she has written, talk to others about the person, study his or her background and education, and, finally, try to secure a personal interview with him or her. The second week do the same with another leader. Continue this procedure until you have studied at least five leaders.
3. Attend speeches given by leaders in your community. Study their good and bad points. Try to decide if any of their speaking techniques would work for you. Do they make mistakes that you wish to avoid?
4. Are you honest in your estimate of how others view you? Watch carefully the "feedback" you get when you are communicating with others (facial expressions, attention, and verbal response). Analyze it for possible clues to others' concept of you. Are others receptive to your ideas or are you fooling yourself by being so "sold" on your ideas that you are blind to their real reactions?
5. Be watchful for evidence of too many judgments in your speech. Try not to criticize others within your group before assessing all the facts. When you are in a group discussion, try to reserve your suggestions and judgments until you have asked for and listened to those of the other members.

6. Are you a democratic or an authoritarian leader? Do you really believe in "government by the people"? Try to exercise democratic leadership even though you may find it a difficult and time-consuming task. Check group response to your democratic leadership. Are the members involved and enthusiastic about their tasks? How would they react to authoritarian leadership?

7. In each communication situation ask yourself: Without regard for who is right or wrong, or whether I like or dislike this person, is there anything I can do to keep the channels of communication open between us until we reach an agreement?

8. Secure a copy of *Parliamentary Procedure: A Programmed Introduction* by Gray and Rea, Scott Foresman Co., 1974, and go through it before you start your business meetings for the year. Secure a copy of *Robert's Rules of Order, Newly Revised* and become familiar enough with it that you can find answers to your parliamentary questions easily and quickly.

9. Take advantage of your community's resources. There are many teachers, principals, lawyers, ministers, physicians, and parents who would be willing to assist you in your leadership tasks. Don't hesitate to ask for help. The advice of some of these people can make up for a lack of experience in working with groups.

Improving Group Skills Within the Council

1. Make the study of group behavior in your council a pleasant hobby. Make the group goals your goals and involve as many people as possible in working toward them. Don't stop with student involvement; get faculty, administration, and parents involved also.
2. Think of two or three groups in which you are an active member. Which can you clearly identify as effective? What factors make one group more effective than another? Could adjustments be made to increase the effectiveness of some groups?
3. Evaluate each meeting for its effectiveness. This is easy to do if you use a member of your group as a "sounding board." After each meeting sit down with this person and talk over the details of the meeting. Ask each other: Was the meeting a success? What contributed to its success (or failure)? What should be changed or repeated at the next meeting?
4. Plan workshops for your group in late summer to prepare for the school year. A workshop in group methods for your committee members is useful. You can include suggestions and practice group problem solving, task recognition, and group planning techniques. This workshop can also serve as an excellent opportunity for the members of your group to get to know each other. A workshop in parliamentary procedure would also be useful to officers and members. The group methods workshop should be one to two full days, while the parliamentary procedure workshop could be accomplished in half a day. Teachers and leaders for these workshops can be found either in your own group and community or from nearby colleges and cities.
5. Groups work better when there is organized activity, a clearly defined and worthwhile goal, and an enthusiastic leader to stimulate and inspire them to work. Try to ensure that these conditions exist in your organization.
6. As you lead group discussions, assist the members by using internal summaries ("Let's take a look at what we have said up to this point"). Word your questions to draw out silent members ("What do you think of that, Jerry?" "Does anyone have information on this subject?" "Have any of you had experiences in situations like this?").
7. Study the following items of "presidential protocol."
    —Go to the outgoing officer and obtain books, files, and records.
    —Never "wise-crack" or play the role of "entertainer" as chairman.
    —Remember to give the floor to the first person who addresses the chair (unless he has had the floor too often and others wish to speak).

—Offer a choice of an important job to the runner-up in the election.
—Praise your fellow officers and committees for their work, but don't seek praise for yourself.
—Attend only those committee meetings where you are directly involved or invited.

Reaching Out to the School Administration and Community

1. Good public relations is essential to an effective student council. This "outreach of goodwill" must go to the student body, faculty, administration, and community. Every effort must be made to gain the cooperation and assistance of these groups. A student council that tries to "go it alone," believing that no one cares or understands, is usually selling its community short. It's true that some groups and individuals are impossible to reach with any program or project, but most are "reachable" with patience and hard work.

2. Try an exercise in role playing. Work up exercises in which members of the council play the roles of faculty members, principal, or chairman of the school board. Communication lines are often opened and strengthened by attempts to view issues from other points of view.

3. Keep your members and school administration informed of your group's activities. In order to make the exchange fair and efficient the administration should inform the student council of actions affecting the student body. Whenever possible, the school administration and the student council should involve each other in their decision-making processes.

4. Rather than imposing his authority on the student council by dominating their meetings or by arbitrarily vetoing their actions, the principal should allow the student council a chance to demonstrate responsibility in conducting its own meetings and deciding questions within its realm of authority. The type of respect most councils seek can only be gained by proving it's a responsible group. This means that most councils must be satisfied with minor issues before the school administration will recognize the group as a mature, decision-making body.

5. Although outbursts of violence in campus demonstrations are effective in gaining newspaper headlines and throwing a degree of fright into the establishment, they seldom solve problems. Anger, ill feelings, resentment, coercion, and brute force rarely create an atmosphere of cooperation. Even if the establishment "gives in" to some of the demands of the moment, there can be no doubt that the experience will instill resentments and fears that will haunt both groups for years to come. Future negotiations will be held in an atmosphere of suspicion and animosity. Every group should, whenever possible, work toward making progress within the atmosphere of good will and understanding.

6. Too many student councils choose to do their favorite activities and aren't representative in their support of student programs

and interests. Often, activities such as student government, student newspaper, debate team, honor society, and fine arts programs appeal to student councils and faculties, over such activities as football, cheerleading, school dances, fraternities, and cake sales. On other occasions, with other councils, the reverse may be true. The point is that each council must make an analysis of how well it represents the interests and needs of the student body as a whole. What kinds of assistance could your council give to worthy student programs that it is not currently supporting?

7. Take every opportunity to make a community contact for your council. Assist the community organizations with their fund drives (volunteers are always needed) and solicit their participation in yours. Make sure the people of the area who aren't parents feel welcome at school performances such as plays and concerts. Make contacts in the local churches, civic clubs, and business groups in order to build your student image and to get an idea of how these groups think and act. In general, make the school activities a part of the total community activity.

8. Remember that "school spirit" includes the academic areas. An effective student council will assist the faculty and administration in promoting academic espirt de corps. This would include the development of a common spirit of enthusiasm, devotion, and respect for class studies. Many schools don't realize how they would profit by having a high academic reputation as a part of their student image. There are many projects the council might consider in this area such as feature stories in the school paper about faculty members and unusual teaching techniques, a "teacher of the year" award, fundraising projects for needed equipment in selected academic areas, an "awards night" to encourage high academic achievement, and promotion of new and better scholarships.

9. Student councils should take a "preventive" approach to problem solving rather than playing the traditional "trouble-shooting" game. The traditional method for determining group tasks in a council is to ask which problems have become serious enough that this year's council should work toward solving them. Although this is an admirable goal and solves some of the difficult problems, it's only a band-aid approach to developing a progressive and ongoing council.

Councils might consider directing at least some of their attention to keeping problems from starting. There isn't as much glory in heading off a possible problem as there is in a tangible solution to an obvious current problem. Some councils are so concerned with their year in office that they fail to work toward preventing next year's problems.

To take a preventive approach, it may be necessary for the council to sacrifice some of the time and effort it would normally spend on current problems. In the long run, however, a council using this approach may make a far more significant and far-reaching contribution to the student body and its welfare. It will require close cooperation between the council, faculty, administration, and community in identifying the possible problem areas, and wise leadership in applying the preventive efforts and making the transition to next year's council. Quality of accomplishment rather than quantity is the real goal.

10. The student council is an ideal opportunity for self-development. This may sound like a selfish goal but it really isn't. Through shared responsibility and accountability a person can gain self-awareness, develop social skills, improve his ability to communicate, develop an appreciation for peer relationships, and gain a working knowledge of the democratic decision-making process.

The best way to promote this self-development is through group work and delegated responsibilities. Officers should see that council decisions are group decisions and not merely the decisions of a few aggressive students. Officers should also delegate the council's work in such a way as to provide opportunities for the council members as well as other interested students. Student involvement helps students develop an identity with their school and its programs.

Tower Building Exercise

Instructions

Choose three to four groups of three to seven members each. All others act as observers. Each group selects a leader.

Brief the leader and observers privately on the following rules and objectives:

1. You will be given a box of Tinker-Toys. The objective is to build the tallest self-supporting structure possible with the contents of the container (you may *not* use the container).
2. You will be allowed a 20-minute planning period. During this time you may *not* assemble pieces. You may dump out the pieces, count them, and handle them, but you may not assemble them by inserting one into any other piece.
3. At the end of the planning period, all pieces must be put back into the container.
4. Next will be a two-minute construction period. The group will only be given starting and stopping times.

Brief the observers privately to note such things as:

1. Leader's behavior.
2. Leader's style.
3. Group's behavior (body language, space, etc.)
4. Adherence or non-adherence to rules.
5. How they keep time and use time effectively.
6. Interpersonal relationships.
7. Group's understanding of the goal.
8. Apathetic, aggressive people.
9. Cooperativeness.
10. People who dominate the task.

Later discussion:

1. Ask observers to cover the items above.
2. Ask members of each group to respond (given sufficient instruction).
3. Ask leaders to respond (frustrations, etc.).

Reading List

Communication Theory

Joseph A. DeVito. *The Interpersonal Communication Book.* New York: Harper & Row, 1983.

Kim Giffin and Bobby Patton. *Fundamentals of Interpersonal Communication.* New York: Harper & Row, 1971.

Blaine Goss. *Communication in Everday Life.* Belmont, Calif.: Wadsworth Co., 1983.

John W. Kelter. *Interpersonal Speech-Communication.* Belmont, Calif.: Wadsworth Co., 1970.

Howard Martin and William Colburn. *Communication and Consensus.* New York: Harcourt Brace Jovanovich, Inc., 1972.

Kenneth K. Sereno and C. David Mortensen. *Foundation of Communication Theory.* New York: Harper & Row, 1970.

One-on-One and Small-Group Communication

Kim Giffin and Bobby Patton. *Problem-Solving Group Interaction.* New York: Harper & Row, 1973.

Thomas A. Harris. *I'm O.K.—You're O.K.* New York: Harper & Row, 1967.

Joyce L. Hocker and William W. Wilmot. *Interpersonal Conflict,* 2nd ed. Dubuque, Iowa: William C. Brown, 1985.

Muriel James and Dorothy Jongeward. *Born to Win.* Menlo, Calif.: Addison-Wesley Co., 1971.

Terry O'Banion and April O'Connell. *The Shared Journey.* Englewood Cliffs, N.J.: Prentice-Hall, 1970.

William S. Smith, *Group Problem-Solving Through Discussion.* New York: Bobbs-Merrill Co., 1965.

Parliamentary Procedure and Public Speaking

J. Jeffrey Auer. *Essentials of Parliamentary Procedure.* New York: Appleton-Century-Crofts, Inc., 1959.

John W. Gray and Richard G. Rea. *Parliamentary Procedure: A Programmed Introduction.* Chicago: Scott Foresman Co., 1970.

Michael Osborn. *Speaking in Public.* Boston, Mass.: Houghton Mifflin Co., 1982.

Loren Reid. *Speaking Well.* New York: McGraw-Hill Co., 1972.

Henry M. Robert. *Robert's Rules of Order, Newly Revised.* Chicago: Scott Foresman Co., 1970.

Wesley Wiksell. *How to Conduct Meetings.* New York: Harper & Row, 1966.

Donald I. Wood. *A Call to Order.* Washington, D.C.: National Association of Secondary School Principals, 1964.

Leadership

C. Argyris. *Increasing Leadership Effectiveness.* New York: Wiley, 1976.

W. G. Bennis. *The Unconscious Conspiracy: Why Leaders Can't Lead.* New York: Wiley, 1982.

D. L. Bradford and A. R. Cohen. *Managing for Excellence: The Guide to Developing High Performance in Contemporary Organizations.* New York: Wiley, 1984.

P. Hersey and K. H. Blanchard. *Management of Organizational Behavior: Utilizing Human Resources,* 4th ed. Englewood Cliffs, N.J.: Prentice-Hall, 1982.

J. G. Hunt and L. L. Larson, eds. *Crosscurrents in Leadership.* Carbondale, Ill.: Southern Illinois University Press, 1979.

B. Kellerman, ed. *Leadership: Multidisciplinary Perspectives.* Englewood Cliffs, N.J.: Prentice-Hall, 1984.

D. E. Lilienthal. *Management: A Humanistic Art.* New York: Columbia University Press, 1967.

M. W. McCall, Jr. and M. M. Lombardo, eds. *Leadership: Where Else Can We Go?* Durham, N.C.: Duke University Press, 1978.

D. McGregor; edited by W. G. Bennis and E. H. Schein, with the collaboration of C. McGregor. *Leadership and Motivation: Essays.* Cambridge, Mass.: M.I.T. Press, 1966.

R. M. Stogdill and Bernard M. Bass. *Stogdill's Handbook of Leadership: A Survey of Theory and Research,* revised and expanded edition) New York: Free Press, 1981.

G. A. Yukl. *Leadership in Organizations.* Englewood Cliffs, N.J.: Prentice-Hall, 1981.